MOTHERHOOD
MODERNITY

MOTHERHOOD AND MODERNITY
An investigation into the rational dimension of mothering

Christine Everingham

Open University Press
Buckingham · Philadelphia

Open University Press
Celtic Court
22 Ballmoor
Buckingham
MK18 1XW

and
1900 Frost Road, Suite 101
Bristol, PA 19007, USA

First Published 1994

A catalogue record of this book is available from the British Library

ISBN 0 335 19195 9 (pb)   0 335 19196 7 (hb)

Typeset by Graphicraft Typesetters Ltd, Hong Kong
Printed in Great Britain by St Edmundsbury Press, Bury St Edmunds, Suffolk

Contents

Acknowledgements   vi

Part one: The mother as subject   1
1 Mothering and feminist theory   3
2 Mothering and morality   20
3 The self in social theory   33

Part two: The study   47
4 The study   49
5 Maternal attitudes   64
6 Taking the attitude of the child   85
7 Maternal attitudes and maternal-infant conflict   99

Part three: Conclusion   117
8 The politics of the particular and the generalized 'other'   119

Notes   136
Bibliography   143
Index   152

Acknowledgements

This book is a revised and shortened version of my PhD thesis. Many people supported and encouraged my efforts during the period of my candidature. My supervisor, Professor John Bern, was a constant source of support and encouragement, giving me fruitful academic guidance and constructive critique. During his academic leave, I was also fortunate enough to have the additional supervision of Associate Professor, Arie Brand. Arie's thorough critique of my work was invaluable in the development of the argument.

I am also indebted to Professor Lois Bryson, Associate Professor Kathryn Robinson and Dr Ellen Jordan for their comments and careful reading of the PhD thesis. The staff from the Department of Sociology and Anthropology at the University of Newcastle, New South Wales, Australia are also to be commended for their encouragement and support over the years.

I would also like to acknowledge the contribution made by Jacinta Evans, the publisher at Open University Press who guided the planning stages of the book and encouraged me to undertake this project.

I have also been fortunate in the support and encouragement that has been given to me by my family, extended family and friends. The insights of the book are embedded in my own experience of mothering and owe much to the close ties that I developed during this time with women who were also mothering. My husband, Michael, also shared in the development of the ideas that flowed from this period, as well as in the many frustrations along the way. My children Rohan, Stefan and Phoebe continue to be a prime source of inspiration, provoking many lateral shifts in thinking from their mother.

I am also deeply indebted to the parents and children who appear in the study, who so willingly let me share in such an important and intimate part of their lives. Our mutual hope is that the effort gone into this project may benefit other parents and children in the future.

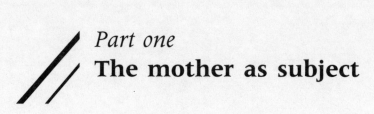

Part one
The mother as subject

1 // Mothering and feminist theory

Introduction

Feminists in the 1960s and early 1970s had a clear objective, equality and greater personal autonomy for women. The major obstacle was mothering. Feminist activists argued very persuasively that women's responsibility for the care of children was responsible for the sexual division of labour and women's position of subordination. If women were to be liberated and achieve equality with men then the ties of motherhood which bound women so closely to the domestic sphere had to be loosened, if not transcended altogether.

During this era, feminists addressing the issue of motherhood took women's autonomy as its critical standpoint. This led to a shift in the focus of investigation from the experience of the child to that of the mother.[1] The claim that mothers had rights and needs of their own provided a standard by which to assess psychological theories of child development. Feminist writers used this standard to highlight the innumerable ways in which psychological theories and models of child development oppressed women, through their failure to consider the mother's separate set of needs and interests.[2]

However, during the late 1970s, the ideal of autonomy which had inspired early second wave feminism came under attack from a new wave of feminist thought. Radical feminists began to question whether this ideal was not, after all, a male construct. Questions were raised as to whether the pursuit of autonomy by women reinforced the traditional male values associated with possessive individualism at the expense of the values of nurturance and connectedness associated with mothering. A new era of feminist writing now attempted to define a specifically female worldview in an attempt to revalue women's specific contribution to society as women. The target of feminist critique shifted from motherhood itself to the social institutions which controlled mothering practices.[3]

The attempt to valorize the contribution of women-as-women to society divided feminist sympathizers. Feminists in the late 1970s, who first confronted this trend towards 'difference', argued that any formulation of women as different to men could be used as a pretext to justify the exclusion of women from the workplace and public life. They feared that any valorization of women's 'difference' could easily be co-opted by conservative interests wanting to confine women to the domestic sphere.[4]

Nevertheless, the majority of women writing from within a feminist perspective today would find it difficult to ignore the insights of radical feminism altogether. The claim that women's difference must inevitably construct a specifically women-centred perspective now appears common place. Moreover, a women-centred perspective is often assumed, at least implicitly, to contain a specifically female value system grounded in an ethics of care and a greater concern for the needs of others. This is a value system which is strongly associated with mothering.

Women writing from within a feminist perspective are confronted with this dilemma. How can the fundamental contribution that women-as-women make to society be specified without tying women's identity to some essentialist notion of what it means to be a woman? Any fixed formulation of women's 'nature' has the potential to undermine women's efforts to achieve some measure of personal autonomy. Yet to ignore women's specific experience as women, and their contribution to society as mothers, inhibits our understanding of nurturing activity and the possible development of a socio-political system grounded in an ethics of care.

This book is concerned with this dilemma. Recent feminist attempts to accommodate the notion of women's difference in feminist perspectives have broadened the notion of difference to include the differences that exist *between* groups of women. This approach has been strongly influenced by poststructuralism and Foucault's analysis of the relationship between knowledge and power. What is brought to the forefront here is the problem of representation, of constructing a single category 'woman' that supposedly represents all groups of women.

These poststructuralist approaches have a number of strengths. They have highlighted the difficulties involved in formulating a broad emancipatory strategy. New questions have been raised. How can any one group of women formulate a political strategy for emancipation that might liberate all women? Is this not simply repeating the mistakes of past grand theorists and revolutionaries who attempted to impose their version of emancipation onto all others? How can a political strategy avoid constructing disadvantaged people as the 'other', the object of social regulation? Indeed, why do we need to develop political strategies at all when all that seems possible is the replacement of one form of oppression with another.[5]

Feminist writers are beginning to address these questions in their attempt to articulate what form a postmodern politics might take.[6] There is a position emerging which has as its cornerstone the proposition that every group of women must be allowed to speak for themselves and construct their own versions of emancipation. The argument here is that feminist theory cannot give direction to a feminist political agenda, since there are no clearly defined goals that can apply to all women. Feminists can only 'listen' to the voices of various women's groups and support a fragmented, directionless agenda at local levels, mobilized around specifically targeted campaigns.[7]

However, this approach to the problem of difference has its own inherent limitations for feminist praxis. It slips easily into a pluralist position where 'anything goes', where critical standards can no longer be upheld. For example, the provision of 'quality' child care is a fundamental demand of feminist organizations. But how can feminists justify what is meant by 'quality' care if there is no value system to refer to, or any model of child development which orientates its knowledge base towards this value system?

At the broader level, an approach to politics which defers to local, special interest groups may discourage feminists from adopting an advocacy role and it may undermine feminist attempts to contribute to the social planning process. The planning process involves the specification of objective criteria of need, orientated towards a value system which cuts across the demands of special interest groups. These specifications cannot be drawn from a poststructuralist perspective.

Feminism does have an emancipatory objective, encompassed by the notion of 'autonomy'. Its own origins are embedded in the project of modernity, defined broadly as the attempt to break free from the constraints of traditional and religious modes of thought. Feminists seek to break away from ascriptive definitions of what it means to be a woman. They seek the freedom to define their own identity. The problem is that feminists cannot take the same route to autonomy that men have taken unless they deny their experience as women and subjugate the values associated with their traditional sphere of activity to the possessive individualism characteristic of public life.[8]

There is, however, an alternative. Rather than reject the project of modernity in its entirety, as many feminists writing from within a poststructuralist position sometimes do, I suggest reworking the notion of 'autonomy' to include women's sphere of activity in a way which does not essentialize the attributes of women. Feminist scholars have already challenged the enlightenment's conception of autonomy, through deconstructing the key dichotomies of nature/culture and mind/body.

These dichotomies frame the enlightenment's vision of autonomy and have been shown to enhance men's emancipation at the expense of constraining women's.[9]

This occurs because the categories of nature/culture and mind/body are portrayed as mutually exclusive and opposing categories. How one category is defined depends upon what it excludes. Since nurturing has strong links to ties of sentiment and the bodies of women and children, it is excluded from the sphere of human agency, or free-will, and placed in the opposite realm of nature. Here, it is seen as a timeless and unalterable activity, guided by natural laws and associated with the natural attributes of women.[10]

The enlightenment's conception of autonomy is grounded in these dichotomous ontologies which essentialize the attributes of women and women's sphere of activity. Dichotomous ontologies have been used in this way as an anchor for social theories, the solid unalterable foundation for the social superstructure. Because women are associated with the fixed, or absolute side of the dichotomy, their sphere of agency and freedom has been constrained, while men's sphere of agency and freedom has been enhanced. Moreover, as feminist scholars have pointed out, dichotomous ontologies 'naturalize' these divisions which are in fact man-made. They have an ideological function.

A central task of this book is to contribute towards the feminist challenge of these dichotomous formulations by clarifying what is actually involved in nurturing activity and its links with a cultural value system orientated towards the enhancement of individual autonomy. But it goes one step further. It also aims to reconstruct the notion of autonomy, to include the agency of women carrying out nurturing activity.

I approach this task by reworking autonomy as a relational concept. The central idea here is that autonomy is a form of subjectivity that is constructed in relation to another's claim to autonomy, in concrete social situations which are imbued with power. This means that autonomy cannot be analysed as a developmental concept, achieved through the acquisition of cognitive and linguistic skills[11] or through the inevitable struggle with an authoritarian father.[12] It is a contingent form of subjectivity that must be actively produced by another in a particular socio-cultural context. In Western society, this 'other' is usually the mother, engaged with the child in nurturing and child-rearing activity. The child's autonomous subjectivity is constructed in relation to the (m)other's own claim to autonomy during this activity.

This understanding of autonomy as an emancipatory form of subjectivity that must be actively constructed in a particular socio-cultural context by a(m)other, whose own claim to autonomy must also be asserted, necessarily involves a rethinking of the notion of human agency. Within the modernity model of the enlightenment thinkers, agency is identified with the public sphere, with collective action guided by generalizable ideals. All those aspects of social life which are not directly responsive to this process of abstraction and generalization have been relegated to the 'sphere of necessity'. Human agency is identified with this specifically created public sphere; mothering is identified with the remainder, 'the sphere of necessity'. The human agent, or subject of history, is all that the mother is not, abstract, generalizable and able to be understood within an instrumental/purposive action framework.[13]

The modernity model of rationality and human agency thereby inhibits our ability to conceive of the mother as a rational being, a critical agent, while engaged in nurturing activity. While nurturing, women are guided by the particularities of their situation. Their decisions are context dependent and embodied, responsive to, and often highly preoccupied with, the affective signals of those around them. Sometimes their reasons for action can be understood from the standpoint of an individual, but often their reasoning takes in the needs of their family as a whole.

If an emancipatory subjectivity needs to be actively constructed by a (m)other during the course of nurturing activity, then nurturing can no longer be allocated to the 'sphere of necessity', where it can be taken for granted as a timeless and unchanging activity guided by natural laws. Moreover, the (m)other moves into focus as a subject, a creator of cultural meanings and human value systems, and her activity becomes a fundamental point of departure for social theories.

The major objective of this book is to draw out the agency of mothers engaged in nurturing activity. The brief review of mothering perspectives below reveals that although a copious amount of material exists on mothering, across the disciplines of psychology, anthropology and sociology, *none* of these works address the rational, or interpretive dimension of nurturing, or orientate their analysis towards considering the significance of maternal-infant conflict in the construction of the child's subjectivity. It is only within feminist perspectives on mothering that the significance of the mother's subjectivity even becomes an issue.

The link with the modernity model of rationality appears throughout these disciplines in the commonly held assumption that the infant's needs are an objective, biological fact. All the mother must do is learn to recognize what the objective requirements of the child are then meet these in the socially prescribed ways. Thus, mothering is a *learning* process, rather than an interpretive and potentially critical act. The learning process may be helped along by 'maternal instinct', but it is essentially a matter of learning to recognize the 'right' meaning of the child's actions and applying the appropriate culturally defined response.

In contrast, the position taken up in this book is that the infant's instinctual expressions cannot be 'known' directly. They must be interpreted and judged by another as expressing a 'need'. It is this process of interpretation and judgement carried out by the mother in a particular 'mothering culture', that in fact structures the child's instinctual impulses as 'needs'.

Moreover, this process of interpretation occurs against the backdrop of the mother's assertion of her own set of needs and interests. The mother's successful assertion of self is not only contingent upon her interpersonal capacities, but on broader, structural factors relating to women in general, such as the status of women in any particular society and the value a particular society attaches to the very notion of autonomy.

The main feature of this book is its portrayal of the interpretive dimension of mothering as a potentially critical act that is guided by a context-dependent and relational notion of autonomy. This is done through an ethnographic study of maternal-infant interaction in three different playgroup settings. What it demonstrates is that mothering is essentially social, involving the mother in a mothering culture that supports and influences her maternal judgements. Moreover, the interpretive activity of the mother is based on an intersubjective social relation that has the potential to coordinate the perspectives of the mother and child in ways that are more or less oppressive to either the mother's or the child's claim to autonomy.

While the primary purpose of the book is to draw out and elaborate the interpretive dimension of mothering, an attempt is also made to consider the implications for feminist theory and political practice. Recognizing the emancipatory potential of mothering does not require us to ignore the agency of women as a collective subject, formulating emancipatory strategies for women at the political level. What is required here is to recognize that the emancipatory activity of women operates at two levels of action.

At the political level, groups representing the special interests of women formulate strategies designed to bring about the institutional changes necessary for women's participation in public life. Here, feminist strategies should focus on making social institutions more responsive to diversity and flexible enough to accommodate the array of solutions worked out by women to meet the demands of their own particular situations. However, women are also agents when they act out their everyday lives. At this level of action, women as sexually specific actors have the opportunity to critically evaluate norms pragmatically, as they are being reproduced in their concrete action context. Further, at this level of action, women as mothers have a critical role to play in their mothering activity. In their daily interaction with their children and peers they are actively constituting cultural meanings and potentially liberating forms of subjectivity.

What the book emphasizes is that mothering involves more than the instrumental act of meeting the child's needs. It also involves more than the imposition of normatively held beliefs and values. The uncovering of the interpretive action of the mother exposes the mother as a critical agent, reflecting upon and responding to, the agency of the child in a particular socio-cultural setting, and in the process, actively constructing cultural meanings and forms of subjectivity within that milieu.

Perspectives on mothering

The social psychology tradition

In the psychological literature, mothering is analysed within a means-end, or instrumental/purposive, action framework. The infant's actions express a 'need' which the mother must learn to recognize and meet with the appropriate, culturally defined response. A stimulus-response mode of communication is set up between the mother and infant, with the mother reading and responding to the cues, or 'signals' of the child.[14]

Brazelton (1974: 73), for example, describes the pattern of communication between the mother and infant in terms of a 'transaction' model, which depicts mothering as a mutual-learning process. Both mother and child must learn 'the nuances of behavior patterns of the other members of the dyad'. These patterns, or 'rules of interaction', are 'constantly being altered by each member of the dyad' so that 'flexibility and change' are necessary for 'maintaining optimal interaction'. One of the first and most important rules concerns the mother's 'sensitivity to the baby's capacity for attention and non-attention'.

The mother must pay 'close attention' to the infant to learn the correct meaning of her infant's cues. Why she should do this is explained with reference to attachment theory, or the inborn capacity of the infant to elicit affection from a primary carer. The crux of attachment theory, developed in the work of John Bowlby (1963), is that the human infant is born into a prolonged state of dependency and must therefore be equipped with biological mechanisms to maintain the proximity of a mother figure. Attachment is the name he gave to the set of behaviours which promote care-giving behaviour.

Attachment gives the infant some control over the care-giving behaviour of the primary carer, which helps to balance out the power of the adult. Power relations are equalized by this ability of the infant to elicit powerful affects in the carer.[15] Using these affective ties, the infant:

> selectively reinforces parent behavior, thus modifying socialization efforts ... It has a set of behaviors which are highly effective in bringing about support, protection, and maintenance of optimum states.
>
> (Bell 1974: 14)

The power of the child to shape care-giving behaviour is also brought out in studies which focus on 'the gaze system'. Stern (1974), for example, describes the development of 'the gaze system' in young infants and reports that infants as young as three to four months use head aversion to terminate intrusive maternal behaviour. The gaze system is also important for securing maternal attention.

In sum, from the social psychology perspective it appears that the infant's actions can be understood rationally from within an instrumental/

purposive action scheme. The child 'knows' what it needs and expresses these needs to the primary carer, who is usually the mother. Gradually, the mother becomes competent at recognizing the 'correct' meaning of the infant's signals.

This perspective portrays mothering as an instrumental act and it is unable to explain why it is overwhelmingly the mother who comes to be the primary carer. However, these studies do have an important contribution to make to our understanding of maternal-infant interaction. Their contribution lies in their detailed documentation of the ability of the child to affect the care-giver through the emotional ties that are generated during the early period of care-giving. The child is said to have agency in the sense that the child shapes care-giving behaviour. There is also a great deal of empirical evidence to support the view that the responsiveness of the care-giver to a particular child builds up during interaction with a particular child over time (Schaffer 1977; Schaffer and Dunn 1979). The implication is that some continuity in care-giving is necessary for the child to realize his or her potential for agency within early care-giving relationships.

More recent discussions of psychological theories of child development have challenged the need for continuity and consistency of care-giving. The volume edited by Beverly Birns and Dale Hay (1988), for example, challenge models of child development which advocate any particular child-rearing practice. Contributors to this volume come from a broad range of disciplines, but they are all women, greatly influenced by second wave feminism and the goal of women's autonomy. Their critique is guided by two broad concerns which reflect this objective.

In the first place, the contributors to this volume are concerned to locate the mother as a separate individual with her own set of needs and interests. Contributors criticize psychological models of child development for their failure to locate the perspective of mothers 'in their own right' (Birns and Hay 1988: 1–2). Their second broad concern hones in on the inability of psychological models to accommodate the diversity of child-rearing patterns that exist cross-culturally and within Western society itself.

For example, after a review of cross-cultural nurturing practices, the contributors, Sarah Sternglanz and Alison Nash (1988: 32) sum up their argument:

> In short, there is no single style of mothering worldwide, or anything close to it . . . In all of these societies, with all of these methods of raising children, children grow up to be normal productive members of their societies.

The emphasis in this volume on accommodating diversity and the perspective of the mother is to be welcomed. It reflects the current trend in social psychology to accommodate the feminist challenge.[16] However,

I approach their way of dealing with the problem of diversity with caution. It cannot justify any critical standard to assess the quality of children's care.

Diversity is accommodated at the expense of accepting anything and everything. It does not appear to matter how children are cared for, so long as they 'grow up to be normal productive members of their societies'. While there does not appear to be any value system guiding their critique of child development models, the contributors of this volume do assume, at least implicitly, that their goal *is* autonomy, at least *women's* autonomy, or autonomy for 'mothers in their own right'. But what child-rearing practices construct an autonomous subjectivity in the child?

Psychological models of child development do, indeed, need to be challenged for their failure to locate the perspective of the mother as a separate individual and their inability to accommodate diversity. Nevertheless, rather than throw all psychological models out, I believe it is more useful to rework them, capturing what they can usefully tell us about child development in relation to the objective of autonomy, but always cautious to situate them within a particular socio-cultural context.

The 'good-enough mothering' model

The 'good-enough' mother is a term first coined by the paediatrician, D.W. Winnicott (1965), and taken over by a number of writers influenced by object-relations psychoanalytic theory, including Harry Guntrip[*] (1969) and Bruno Bettelheim (1987). In this model, the mother is seen as an 'optimal frustrator', who provides a care-giving environment for the child that minimizes the child's negative emotional experiences. The good-enough mother knows instinctively, or through 'empathy', what the needs of her child are and adapts her behaviour to meet these needs as they develop and express themselves.

Once again, *how* the mother comes to 'know' what the needs of her child are is simply assumed, or else explained by way of casual references to nature or bodily affects. Because the underlying assumption here is that the child's needs are a biological, objective fact, writers within this tradition have come to believe that the mother can create a 'near perfect care-giving environment' simply through meeting these needs. They are also able to specify what this ideal care-giving environment would be. It is one in which the child's experiences of 'bad' object relations are minimal.

Followers of this tradition tend to advocate such an ideal setting. Winnicott, for example, is an object relations writer who depicts the image of a 'good-enough mother' as one who minimizes the negative emotional experiences of her child. According to Guntrip (1969: 44), Winnicott regards the infant's needs as so absolute at first as to require a 'perfect' environment in theory, and as near perfect as is attainable in practice:

This 'perfect' environment is provided by the mother who actively adapts to the infant's needs as they develop and are expressed. Her maternal intuition recognises and provides what the baby wants as and when he wants it.

Infants' needs are thereby defined by the laws of nature, and they unfold and express themselves according to these laws. The good-enough mother will soon become attuned to this natural process and allow her child to develop in accordance with 'his own inner nature and laws of growth' (Guntrip 1969: 44).

Cross-cultural perspectives

There is an anthropological tradition that also takes the needs of the infant as given in biology. Infants have certain biologically given needs which mothers meet in culturally prescribed ways. Diversity between cultures is the outcome of different cultural prescriptions for meeting basic human needs. The most influential example of this tradition is Margaret Mead, one of the first anthropologists to focus on child-rearing activity. In her Introduction to *Childhood in Contemporary Cultures*, she makes a clear distinction between biology (natural and universal) and culture (man-made and particular). While it is possible to begin with certain biological givens, 'of what all beings have in common', the study of anthropology focuses on the diverse ways in which different cultures organize their societies to meet these basic human needs.

Cross-cultural research into child-rearing practices undertaken by social psychologists during the 1960s and 1970s were also based on the nature/culture, mind/body dichotomies.[17] However, more recent anthropological work is critical of the idea that biology takes a fixed, universal form. The biological basis of attachment theory, for example, has been critically assessed by Nancy Scheper-Hughes (1985). Her essay 'Culture, scarcity and maternal thinking: maternal detachment and infant survival in a Brazilian shantytown', demonstrates the impact of the material environment on ideas relating to care-giving behaviour. Her study demonstrates that care-giving behaviour is shaped by other important factors, apart from the actions of the child. It thereby undermines the universal applicability of the biological explanations for mothering given in 'attachment' models.

In the community studied by Scheper-Hughes, mothers suffer extreme poverty. Attachment does not necessarily form between mother and child, even if the mother is in close contact with the infant from birth and breast-feeds. The weaker, more passive babies are not highly regarded and are selectively neglected by their poverty stricken mothers. The community of mothers have developed an ideology that helps to legitimate this neglect, through envisaging life as a power struggle between strong and weak. Passive, non-demanding infants are believed to lack a drive towards life, so that it is thought best that the weaker babies die young, 'without a prolonged and wasted struggle' (Scheper-Hughes 1985: 304). Scheper-Hughes' point is that ideas, grounded in the mother's material conditions of existence, have a powerful role to play in the shaping of care-giving behaviour.

The biological basis of care-giving behaviour comes under a sustained challenge from anthropologists influenced by feminism. This body of research demonstrates the importance of the socio-cultural context in shaping care-giving behaviour. Annette Hamilton's study of child-rearing practices on an Aboriginal settlement in North-Central Arnhem Land, for example, shows how the mother's attitude towards caring for her infant is affected by the attitudes of others in the community.

Hamilton (1981: 34) points out that the social life of the Anbarra camp would seem to provide the best possible conditions for multiple mothering. She observes, however, that in fact this community strives 'to maximise the exclusivity of the mother–child bond'. Young children in this community are very dependent on their own mothers. This relation of dependence seems to have its origins in the fact that in this community, as in other Aboriginal communities that have been studied by anthropologists (Malinowski 1963), crying babies agitate adults to such an extent that the crying is immediately averted. Since the only response to a crying baby is to put the baby to the breast until the crying abates, mothers experience strong group pressure to attend to their own babies.

Studies which highlight the socially constructed nature of care-giving activity are able to demonstrate that mothering practices are contingent and therefore receptive to social change. However, what, exactly, needs to be changed in our mothering practices to produce a more emancipated society still needs to be spelt out, along with a clearer picture of how social change is actually effected.

The feminist focus on mothering

The feminist focus on mothering came after a period of sociological interest in the 'family', largely influenced by the work of Talcott Parsons and role theory. Under the impact of second wave feminism, the focus of investigation underwent a dramatic shift. The object of investigation became the experience of motherhood, from the point of view of the mother. This was a dramatic reversal of studies into infant care that were intent on discovering the effect of mothering on the child.

These early feminist works on motherhood did not investigate the dynamics of mothering, their primary goal being to bring to light the hereto neglected experience of the mother. The in-depth interview was the preferred method, with feminist sociologists conveying the subjective experience of mothers through verbatim reports.[18] Feminists who did focus more on the dynamics of mothering did so through analysing professional discourses on mothering. These were criticized for neglecting the rights and needs of mothers, for creating unreal expectations of the mothering role and for making mothering into a very stressful occupation.[19]

During the 1970s and 1980s, feminist writing took a theoretical turn. Women's position of subordination was identified with their mothering role. Theoretical models were developed to explain women's willingness to mother and participate in their own oppression. There were two broad explanatory approaches to the problem of why women were willing to mother and participate in their own oppression; ideological and psychosocial.

Analyses which stressed the importance of ideology focused on those ideas about mothering that reinforced the notion that mothers should be responsible for the care of their own children. Betsy Wearing's (1984) Australian study of mothers illustrates this approach. Wearing's work reveals how women experience motherhood in contemporary Western society. Mothering activity is regarded as tedious and extremely demanding, rewarding yet often exhausting and emotionally draining. It also limits the mother's attempts to enter the public world and find greater self-fulfilment. Wearing's interviews focus on tenets of the 'good' mother, those belief systems which inhibit the mother's attempts to organize alternative child care arrangements which might relieve the pressures of mothering and allow mothers to achieve some measure of independence.

Wearing's work demonstrates the usefulness of being able to employ the critical standard of women's autonomy to an analysis of mothering activity. However, the usefulness of this standard is limited by the assumptions about human agency that are implicit in Wearing's theoretical framework. It remains grounded in the modernity, or 'transcendence' model of human agency. Thus, mothering is evaluated in terms of how it inhibits women's efforts to control social institutions and achieve independence and self-fulfilment in public life. While this perspective has made a valuable contribution to women's emancipatory struggles, it occludes a perspective that might draw out the contribution that mothers make to the creation of value systems and forms of subjectivity through their nurturing activity.

Wearing's theoretical perspective implicitly takes on the assumptions about human agency embedded in the modernity model. Nurturing activity appears to be carried out in an asocial, 'domestic' space located somewhere outside culture. Cultural values appear to be constituted in the public sphere. Groups of mothers have no potential to shape cultural meanings through their nurturing activity; they simply reinforce cultural values defined by men and public institutions. Mothering in contemporary Western society reinforces 'the traditional ideas concerning motherhood, sex-roles, etc.' (Wearing 1984: 39).

The feminist trend to implicitly evaluate mothering in terms of the modernity paradigm is demonstrated in another volume concerned with mothering, edited by Joyce Trebilcot. According to Trebilcot (1984:

1), mothering 'typical' of patriarchal societies 'helps to perpetuate' the dominant values and hierarchical arrangements of that society. Mothers are 'expected to transmit' these values during socialization and are required to support the patriarchal system through their caring activity.

Trebilcot's strategy for feminist activists is to work at the institutional level, to restructure day-to-day child care so that this is not 'the primary responsibility of mothers and their female relatives'. A central theme of the book is the notion that 'it is reasonable, or even required, for women to withdraw from mothering' (p. 3). There is no opening here to locate the mother as a critical agent, questioning, assessing and creating value systems as they reproduce these in their everyday life context.

Yet Trebilcot (1984: 3) is also aware of the need to integrate women's concerns regarding the realization of their own women-centred values and 'women-identified forms of life' into feminist strategies. She includes in the volume essays which focus on women's positive contribution to a more nurturing and caring society. Where, then, do these values of nurturance and concern for others come from? Are they 'natural', an essential female condition? How is it that women can have a distinctive set of values, grounded in mothering activity if mothers have no agency – if mothering is located outside culture and morality?[20]

Sara Ruddick's essay on 'Maternal thinking' points to a possible solution to this problematic. According to Ruddick (1982: 77), mothering is a discipline involving judgements of success and failure. It is a particular mode of rationality, remaining connected to the body, that involves the mother as a critical agent, 'establishing criteria for determining failure and success, in setting the priorities, and in identifying the virtues and liabilities the criteria presume'.

However, despite Ruddick's disclaimer that her description of 'maternal thinking' is culturally specific (p. 78), there remains the danger that this mode of maternal thinking be construed as universal, and therefore natural, or an essential attribute of women. If the concept is to be useful for feminist theory and praxis then the moral dimension of this particular mode of maternal thinking needs to be drawn out and analysed. As it stands, Ruddick's concept of maternal thinking lacks any way for this particular mode of mothering to be analysed as a socio-cultural construct. In this book, I re-conceptualize the notion of 'maternal thinking' as 'maternal attitudes' that require both empirical description and analytical explanation.

This approach maintains the critical standpoint of women's autonomy, although the concept of autonomy is thoroughly reworked from within a relational perspective that considers how the child's autonomy is structured in relation to the mother's. Since it attempts to provide a critical standard, it can be contrasted with a current trend to integrate the insights of the postmodern era through perspectives influenced by Foucault's conception of power.[21]

Valerie Walkerdine and Helen Lucey (1989) illustrate this position.

They review the data taken from a psychological study which explores the relationship between specific maternal attitudes and the child's cognitive and linguistic achievements at school. This was a study which had tried to demonstrate the importance of mothering in child development. The authors of the original study had attempted to draw out the characterics of a 'sensitive mother' which would enhance the cognitive development of the child and ensure that the child developed into a responsible citizen, capable of participating in Western, democratic culture.

Walkerdine and Lucey re-interpret this data in the light of Foucault's analysis of the relationship between knowledge and power. The use of this framework allows them to go far beyond previous analyses of mothering which utilized the ideal of women's autonomy to criticize psychological models. It is not just the fact that these models elicit unrealistic expectations in mothers, nor that they reinforce beliefs about children needing their mothers in constant attendance. Their analysis goes much further; psychological models are in themselves regulatory. They construct a worldview which governs mothering activity. Mothers are managed through these psychological discourses, which repress potential forms of conflict and any basis for resistance.

Walkerdine and Lucey (1989: 25) argue that the construction of the ideal of the sensitive mother through psychological discourse reinforces the fundamental illusion of our democratic culture, that people have agency and control over their lives. The sensitive mother who works at constructing an 'autonomous child' is merely reinforcing this illusion. It is simply an 'elaborate charade'.

While a sensitive mother might believe she is empowering her child, in reality she is being managed by a discipline which leads her to hide 'the fear, the spectre of authoritarianism, or rebellion which ensue if the child realizes herself to be powerless' (p. 24). By repressing the very real conflict of interests that exist, the mother is not empowering the child, but undermining the possibility of the child's resistance to power:

> She turns resistance and even violence from her children into 'feelings' that make themselves and others unhappy and she rationalizes it so that it has no force.
>
> (p. 25)

What is oppressive about the construction of the ideal of 'the sensitive mother' is the repression of maternal-infant conflict and the opportunities conflict provides for resistance. Does this mean, then, that a model which encourages women to assert their own set of interests over the child's is less oppressive to women and children?

This would appear to be the case, since these authors have a more positive evaluation of the mothering attitudes of working-class women who allow their power struggles to become explicit:

> If the child interferes [with the mother's domestic work], she can be told not to be demanding, be told off. In this way the mother

makes her power explicit, especially her power to withhold her attention . . . This makes possible explicit power struggles . . . and they are much more likely *successfully* to resist the child's demands. They do not use such instances as regulative devices.

(p. 78)

Although working-class mothers are still regulated, it is a different form of regulation. They are regulated by the pragmatic, or material demands of their everyday life existence. The authors appear to find this form of regulation less oppressive than the regulation of middle-class mothers by professional discourse, since this latter form of regulation stifles conflict and the opportunity for resistance.

But do Walkerdine and Lucey mean to imply that the child is *always* powerless, and that any attempt made by the mother to empower the child is inherently illusory? Does it matter what attitude the mother adopts towards the child, so long as she doesn't try to repress conflict? Does the repression of maternal-infant conflict via the 'democratic' model of child-rearing have the same effect as repressing resistance through authoritarian child-rearing attitudes?

I do not believe that these questions can be addressed from within a theoretical framework that regards all social relations as power relations and all aspects of the child's agency as illusory. An alternative approach to the role of professional expertise has been suggested by Kerreen Reiger (1985). Rather than see the expansion of professional expertise as undermining any possibility for emancipation, her work on the modernization of the Australian family demonstrates that the expansion of professional expertise has had contradictory outcomes for the cause of women's emancipation.

Reiger argues that an important outcome of the extension of professional expertise was the undermining of bourgeois assumptions as to the 'naturalness' of women's domestic and nurturing activity. While she has little doubt that the modernization of the Australian family placed a tremendous burden on parents, and the mother in particular, she leaves us to consider the 'emancipatory moment' that the process of modernization set in train. This moment has been opened up through the increasing acceptance of domestic and nurturing activity as a social, rather than a natural phenomenon. The knowledge base of professional expertise thereby has the potential to undermine the dichotomies of mind/body, nature/culture, public/private on which men constructed their version of liberty, at the expense of women's. Thus, rather than work solely with a conception of human agency as 'resistance' to forms of domination, Reiger's work suggests the need to adopt a position more sensitive to the contradictions inherent in the process of modernization and more informed as to the active contribution made by women, as mothers and as welfare activists, to the overall emancipatory project.

In this book, I take up Reiger's challenge to explore the agency of women and rework Habermas' notion of an intersubjective social relation to locate the mother as a subject, guided by an emancipatory ideal. This enables me to clarify two separate perspectives, the child's and the mother's. How mothers coordinate these perspectives is the focus of the ethnographic study. While maternal-infant conflict remains a central concern, so too are the different ways in which these two perspectives are coordinated.

Psychoanalytic feminism

Feminists have also approached the problem of women's subordination through psychoanalytic perspectives. Nancy Chodorow's influential *Reproduction of Mothering* (1978) utilized object-relations psychoanalytic theory to explain why women continued to mother in terms of the different psychic development that occurred in boys and girls as a result of being mothered by women. While her theory provided a rationale for involving men in nurturing, it did not at this stage address the question of the mother as a subject. This theme was developed to a much greater extent in her later essay, 'Beyond drive theory: object-relations and the limits of radical individualism' (Chodorow 1985), where she critically assesses psychoanalytic theory for its inability to locate the mother as a separate subject.

Adopting Habermas' notion of intersubjectivity, Chodorow is able to depict the subjectivity of the mother as the crucial factor in determining how the child comes to desire the move away from primary narcissism to autonomy. The mother's assertion of self structures the child's drives in a way that includes recognition of the 'claims for pleasure' of others. While we can now see that the mother's actions *determine* in some fundamental way the structuring of the child's sense of autonomy, we are no closer to understanding how or why the mother's 'assertion of self' actually occurs. Can we regard the mother's assertion of herself as a separate being, with a claim to autonomy, as a universal?

Jessica Benjamin's book *The Bonds of Love* (1990) also co-opts Habermas' concept of an intersubjective social relation to locate the mother as a separate subject. In her work, Benjamin attempts to provide an alternative to the internalization of paternal authority as the only route to authentic personal autonomy. Benjamin adopts Kohut's concept of 'recognition' connecting it to the intersubjective perspective of Habermas to depict 'mutual recognition' as the mechanism whereby the child achieves autonomy.

However, while Benjamin (1990: 19–20) acknowledges the origins of the intersubjective view in Habermas' theory, her use of the concept loses the notion of intersubjectivity as an interpretive act which is central in Habermas' formulation of communicative action. She does not focus on the question of *how* the mother comes to 'know' and recognize her child. Instead, she begins from the premise that recognition is a 'need', that mothers have the capacity to fulfil. Recognition begins with '. . . the mother's ability to identify and respond to her infant's physical needs, her "knowing her baby", when he wants to sleep, eat, play alone, or play together' (pp. 22–3).

Mutual recognition is also a 'need':

> The idea of mutual recognition is crucial to the intersubjective view; it implies that we actually have a need to recognise the other as a separate person who is like us yet distinct. This means that the child has a need to see the mother, too, as an independent subject, not simply as the 'external world' or an adjunct of his ego.
>
> (p. 23)

The implication is that the actual mechanism involved in the process of mutual recognition is a need. In asserting their own subjectivity, the mother and child are simply fulfilling each other's need for recognition. The need for mutual recognition causes a tension between recognition of (m)other on the one hand, and assertion of self on the other. Benjamin argues that mutual recognition is constituted in this tension, which must be maintained for the child to develop an adequate conception of self that is self-fulfilling as well as considerate of others.

Although she is unable to offer an adequate explanation of the actual mechanism involved in achieving 'recognition', Benjamin's work does elucidate the importance of recognizing the two perspectives that are involved in the early care-giving relationship and the centrality of conflict, as well as the state of 'connectedness', or 'symbiosis', usually associated with mothering in the psychoanalytic literature.

This brief review of perspectives on mothering uncovers the central questions addressed in this book. *How* does the mother come to 'know' what it is her infant 'needs'? How does she coordinate her own set of interests and needs with those of the child? What contribution does the nurturing process make to the construction of value systems and the child's subjectivity?

2 / Mothering and morality

Is nurturing natural?

Nurturing is associated with the idea of nourishment, of satisfying the basic emotional and physical requirements of young children. Social theorists have elaborated very little on this common-sense understanding of nurturing, even though they have relied on nurturing activity to provide the bedrock for their theories of socialization. Nevertheless, although nurturing has escaped rigorous sociological investigation, theories of socialization contain a number of implicit assumptions about nurturing activity that need to be drawn out if the socio-cultural dimension of nurturing activity is to be fully understood. All of these assumptions are associated with the belief that nurturing is natural.

Assumption 1: nurturing is an instrumental act
The belief here is that the child's emotional and physical needs are an objective reality, given in their biological and physiological make-up. What mothers do in their nurturing activity is to satisfy (or frustrate) these needs in the appropriate, culturally defined ways. How the mother comes to know the needs of her child is thought to be a learning process, a process of trial and error. This may be of interest to psychologists, but not to sociologists, since the mother is only a means to an end.

An important consequence of this first assumption is that nurturing is not analysed as part of the socialization process as such, but as a separate and *prior* process. Nurturing is essential for the child's physical survival and it transmits the basic, *unsocialized* emotion of 'love'. This emotion of 'love' provides the 'instinctual base' for the development of the socialized emotions, which occurs at a later stage.[1]

Assumption 2: motherly love is unsocialized

The assumption that nurturing is an instrumental activity is linked to a second and related assumption, that the emotions that pass between the mother and infant are a product of their biological make-up. They are not socialized emotions and so do not appear to have a value component. Motherly love, for example, although understood to be the foundation on which personality structure is built, is regarded as instinctive, a natural bi-product of maternal-infant interaction.

An important consequence of this assumption is that it overlooks the socialization of maternal-infant emotions. The mother's contribution to social life is believed to be natural, timeless and unalterable. It is the emotional 'complex' associated with 'guilt' that is regarded as the product of civilization. Love and compassion, transmitted to the child through early maternal-infant interaction, are simply products of nature.[2]

Assumption 3: nurturing is carried out in a private space

The belief here is that nurturing is a social act carried out between the mother and child. The mother and child are viewed as a single, interactive unit, or dyad. The mother interprets the child's actions functionally, by correctly identifying the child's intentions. Thus, there is no apparent need for the mother to refer to her socio-cultural milieu to identify the meaning of the child's actions.

This view of how the mother derives meaning from within the dyad itself is strongly associated with the idea that social life is either 'private' or 'public'. Despite years of criticism by feminist writers, the public/ private distinction remains fundamental to the theoretical frameworks of contemporary theories of socialization. Within the confines of these categories, nurturing activity loses its social character.

Parsons' (1956) model of the isolated nuclear family remains an important influence here. He depicted the nuclear family as isolated in the sense that it was a self-sustaining sub-system, with the parents no longer dependent upon kin or outside supports. Moreover, he believed that this family type was necessary for the construction of the personalities needed by Western industrialized society.

In creating this personality structure, mothers and fathers had clearly defined roles, prescribed by society. The mother's role was 'expressive', that is, highly personalized and emotive and concerned with the internal maintenance of the relationships within the family. He depicted the father's role as lying along the 'instrumental' axis, with his role as breadwinner linking the family sub-system to society at large. The expressive axis required the mother to 'love' her child, but also to 'understand rationally the nature, conditions and limitations of that love and the ways in which its deviant forms can injure rather than benefit her child' (Parsons and Bales 1956: 26). Thus, the expressive action by the mother did involve her in making judgements about her emotional exchanges with the child, but Parsons seemed to believe that these judgements could be carried out by the mother in a self-referencing system, within the mother-infant dyad itself, in isolation from her kin and community of peers. It was through the instrumentally defined role of the father that the family sub-system linked up with the rest of society (Parsons and Bales 1956: 47).

Feminist scholars have convincingly challenged Parsons' view of the family as a self-sustaining sub-system. It is clear that women remain very dependent upon outside supports, particularly while they are nurturing pre-school age children.[3] Nevertheless, despite the feminist challenge, the assumptions built into Parsons' model are still influencing the way in which many sociologists understand the socialization process. It still seems to be implicitly assumed, for example, that nurturing consists of instrumental acts carried out by isolated mothers who respond to the biological drives of their children according to their culturally prescribed role of 'mother'.

The point is that this way of understanding the social ignores what we know about the actual social space in which nurturing takes place. Furthermore, what it assumes to be the norm is in fact pathological. Some mothers are indeed 'isolated' from any communal supports while they are nurturing, but this condition needs to be seen as a pathological condition for a nurturing mother, likely to cause the mother great stress. It is more often the case that mothers become intensely involved in social networks while nurturing.

By placing mothering activity in a private, rather than social space, the attitude adopted by mothers towards their nurturing activity can easily be dismissed as a matter for each woman's own, individual 'taste', or perhaps 'competence'. The way in which nurturing activity is regulated, or socially constituted and constrained is occluded. The feminist challenge to the public/private distinction focus on this problem. Their critique draws out the way in which motherhood ideals are shaped by the structural constraints of the public sphere. But feminist theory still lacks the conceptual tools necessary to investigate the contribution of maternal-infant interaction and the 'mothering culture' to the *construction* of value systems. This can be seen, for example, in the way that many feminist writers continue to use the categories of public/private, even if they regard them as 'interdependent', rather than separate and opposed.[4]

Although 'interdependent', the sphere in which mothering is carried out is still often assumed to be the isolated, domestic space portrayed by Parsons. Although regarded as socially constructed rather than governed by natural laws, there is still a tendency to work with the categories of 'public' and 'private', or perhaps 'domestic'. Thus, nurturing activity still appears as a functional act, carried out primarily by individual mothers acting within the confines of the domestic household, despite the empirical evidence that women become very involved in interpersonal networks while nurturing.

These assumptions need to be challenged if the value system associated with nurturing activity is to be seen as socially constructed, rather than an essential attribute of women. The problem is, that these assumptions are so embedded in sociological theory that it is impossible to use any conventional conceptual tools to analyse the social dimension of nurturing. Each concept must be carefully examined for the way in which it occludes the subjectivity of the mother.

The most immediate problem is to describe a sphere of action in which nurturing can take place, which is social. Tönnies' classic distinction between *Gemeinschaft* and *Gesellschaft*, that is, community and association, provides an alternative conception of the social which is a worthwhile starting point. Rather than using the categories of 'public' and 'private' to analyse all social activity, Tönnies' analyses social activity according to the predominant organizing principle of the action involved. He used the concepts of *Gemeinschaft* and *Gesellschaft* to typify this difference.

The most useful insight which comes out of the following discussion of Tönnies' work is that action cannot always be explained with reference to the intentions of the isolated individual actor. In kinship and communal groupings, action is often geared towards maintaining the solidarity of the group. Actors in these forms of social organization are not individuated, in that they are living out their lives in conditions of varying degrees of interpersonal dependence. This means that actors in communal forms of social organization very often have a number of competing concerns to consider. Their action reflects their efforts to coordinate these competing interests and concerns, rather than a specific goal.

Morality in communal forms of social organization

Gemeinschaft *and* Gesellschaft

The fundamental difference between the ties of *Gemeinschaft* and the ties of *Gesellschaft* is that *Gemeinschaft* consists of an organic, or unified, community where the actions of individuals are an end in themselves. They maintain the unity of the group. In the *Gesellschaft*, on the other hand, each individual acts in isolation, according to self-interest, or a specified purpose. Individuals within *Gemeinschaft* forms of social organization act to maintain the unity of the group. Individuals within *Gesellschaft* forms of social organization are unified through a common purpose.

In Tönnies' (1957: 37) view, the unity of *Gemeinschaft* is the original human condition. Its origins lie in necessity, the fact of human dependence. Actors are linked to each other through 'parental descent and by sex, or by necessity become so linked'. This means that in *Gemeinschaft*, action cannot be understood within a teleological action scheme. It is not the goal of the action that integrates the community, but the action itself, as this action reflects relations of mutual reciprocity and interdependence.

My interpretation of Tönnies' notion of an organic community of people united through necessity is that the binding power of the bond between members of this community must remain tied to the particularities, or personal characteristics, of its members. One individual is not interchangeable with another, since the personal attributes of members is crucial to the ties that unite the group. Ties of sentiment are not transferable.[5]

In the *Gesellschaft*, however, it is the goal of the action which unifies the community, rather than the action itself. Human wills are 'mechanically', or 'artificially' unified through the goals of their association. The personal characteristics of actors are not relevant to the binding power of their association. As far as the integration of their association is concerned, these actors are interchangeable with others who accept the terms of the contract, since the binding power of their tie lies outside individual members, in the code of conduct which defines their rights and responsibilities (Tönnies 1957: 64–5).

Tönnies' used the concept of will, or volition, to depict the fundamental force behind action in any human society. He developed the concept of 'natural will'[6] to depict the will of the members of *Gemeinschaft* and he opposed this concept to that of 'rational will', characteristic of the will of members of *Gesellschaft*. According to Tönnies' dichotomy, each type of will has a different relationship to the mind, or 'thinking'. The 'natural will' does have a 'thinking' component, that is to say it is linked to the mind, but in the opposite direction to the 'thinking' component of rational will (1957: Part 2).

Natural will reaches the mind by way of the body, where it originates. The action it invokes concretizes the sensations of the body that have been brought to the mind. The thinking associated with the natural will is immanent in the action, rather than expressing some future goal. It is tied, therefore, to the past and takes on the forms of 'liking', 'habit' and 'memory' (pp. 108–14).

The thinking involved in the rational will, however, is *prior* to the act. It originates in the mind, rather than the body and can therefore project into the future. The thinking of the rational will maintains a separate identity to the activity it thinks about. It has an imaginary, rather than concrete, existence. In the ideal case, the thought of the end, or goal, dominates all other considerations. The rational will takes on the forms of 'deliberation', 'discrimination' and 'conceptualization' (pp. 121–5).

Tönnies formulated his distinctions as ideal types. The concepts were abstractions to which real societies, and the actual wills of real people, could be compared. All societies contained both *Gemeinschaft* and *Gesellschaft* components, with their associated form of will, but they could be described by the extent to which they exhibited tendencies towards these two types (p. 249). He also applied his concepts to the historical process as a sequential development. The *Gemeinschaft*, with its essential unity, is logically prior to the development of *Gesellschaft* and diversity. *Gesellschaft* emerges within, out of and alongside *Gemeinschaft*. Modernity is envisaged as the sequential displacement of *Gemeinschaft* with *Gesellschaft*, the pathological condition of which is the separation of the means from the subject of action:

> the means develop their own logic and lawfulness and men must obey them, even if they continue to live in the illusion that they are the masters and the means are the servants and instruments. The power of the isolated means over human thoughts and actions is the hallmark of the spirit of modernity.
>
> (Tönnies 1973: 282–3)

Tönnies' pathology of societal rationalization is a form of alienation, or mode of estrangement of humankind from their own activity. The development of *Gesellschaft* focuses human effort on the best possible techniques to achieve a certain goal. This leads to a sharp division between means and ends. The means have their own logic which ultimately determines action (Mitzmann 1973: 10).

However, Tönnies (Salomon 1973: 45) does suggest the possibility of an alternative outcome. Reason could develop into a new form with these changes, and reconstruct *Gemeinschaft* in a new type of social relationship based on a conscious ethic, but reason must first develop to the stage where it can reunite the rational with the organic, the analytical with the creative. Reason must become a 'healing force of the community'.[7]

Gemeinschaft *deconstructed*
Where, though, did Tönnies' imagine this 'healing force' could come from? To answer this question, Tönnies was forced to look back, somewhat nostalgically, to the communal life that had existed in his childhood. Central to this communal life were the traits of women, the 'joy of intuition and love'.[8] Because of his dichotomous categorizations, he was forced to assume that the missing attributes needed to be injected into society were part of the biological make-up of women.[9]

He did foresee the entry of women into the workforce and public life, believing that this would hasten the end of *Gemeinschaft* and the atomization of society into individual units more than any other single factor (Tönnies 1957: 166). However, he also suggested that the entry of women into public life might provide the necessary ingredients for the reunification of the rational with the organic and the reconstruction of *Gemeinschaft*. This could happen as women developed a common 'group consciousness', enabling them to 'rise' to a 'moral-humane consciousness' (p. 166).

By attributing the missing attributes to the biological make-up of women, Tönnies avoided having to analyse where the values associated with nurturance and concern for others came from. He was able to solve the paradox of modernity through assuming that women would take these character traits with them when they entered public life. All that was required was for women to generalize their particular attributes to their *Gesellschaft* relations.

Tönnies' solution to the paradox of modernity highlights the fundamental problem with his scheme of the social. Feminists have pointed out that women's character traits are socially constructed. There is no necessary link between women and the values associated with care and nurturance. If we continue to use dichotomous constructs which place the mind and body, nature and culture in mutually exclusive and opposing categories it will be impossible to explain where the values associated with nurturance and compassion come from.

At this point, contemporary feminists have an important contribution to make. Their deconstructive efforts have brought the whole question of the relationship between reason and nature, the mind and the body into focus. Feminists have argued that reason and the body, like nature and culture, have been separated *conceptually* as binary oppositions.[10] They are man-made conceptual constructs which do not necessarily reflect their real life forms. Modernity as a paradox is the logical outcome of using dichotomous models of nature and culture, mind and body, reason and sentiment.

Nevertheless, if we keep the feminist critique of dichotomous categorizations in mind, it is possible to gain some useful insights into the moral dimension of communal forms of social organization from Tönnies' work. In particular, we can utilize Tönnies' fundamental insight that there are different organizing principles that regulate social life, depending upon whether or not actors are already individuated. If actors in a community are not individuated, there exists a need to maintain the relationships of the group. Action here is regulated in a fundamentally different way to action regulated in associative forms of social organization, where the actors are individuated and united through impersonal 'codes of conduct'.

The aspect of moral regulation peculiar to communal forms of social organization has been overlooked by later social theorists, including Weber and more recently Habermas. Parsons has attempted to draw out the moral dimension of communal forms of organization, realizing that Weber had overlooked this when he coopted Tönnies' notion of *Gemeinschaft* and *Gesellschaft*. I shall discuss Parsons' elucidation of the moral dimension of *Gemeinschaft* and return to apply the feminist critique of dichotomous constructs to Parsons' interpretation of Tönnies' work.

Parsons' elucidation of the moral element of Gemeinschaft

Both Weber and Parsons have acknowledged the influence of Tönnies' *Gemeinschaft/Gesellschaft* distinction on their respective action-theoretical models.[11] However, when discussing the origins of his action scheme,

Parsons (1973: 140) goes back to Tönnies' fundamental distinction, rather than Weber's action categories. Parsons does this to elucidate an important difference between his own and Weber's action models. This difference has to do with the way in which Weber excluded the moral element from *Gemeinschaft*.

Parsons agrees with Weber that the norms of *Gemeinschaft* may best be described as modes of expression of *attitudes* rather than as means to specific ends. However, he disagrees with Weber's view that this means that *Gemeinschaft* norms can be analysed in the same way as Weber's concept of *Brauch*, that is 'norms of taste'. In Parsons' view, *Gemeinschaft* norms are not just subjectively experienced and expressed, but they involve moral elements that are institutionally enforceable.[12]

According to Parsons, there is a fundamental difference between the way in which obligations are enforced in *Gemeinschaft* and *Gesellschaft*. In *Gesellschaft*, obligations are limited to the terms of the contract, which must be accepted by members who enter into the association. They can be enforced by sanction if necessary. In the *Gemeinschaft*, however, obligations are typically unspecified and unlimited. If specified at all, it is only in very general terms which reflect the proper *attitude* to adopt. For example:

> in the marriage oath each assumes the obligation to 'love and cherish, for richer, for poorer, in sickness and in health'. It is a blanket obligation to help in whatever contingency may arise in the course of a common life.
>
> (Parsons 1973: 144)

Although the *Gemeinschaft* does not explicitly state all the rules of conduct, Parsons believes that there is nevertheless a system of institutional control:

> But it does not in general take the form of norms directly regulating the specific ends, means and conditions of actions within the relationship. Where this occurs it is generally at the periphery. Certain things will be regarded as indispensable minima for the relationship to exist at all . . . institutional sanction is concerned rather with attitudes than with specific acts. The latter are judged primarily as expressions of these attitudes.
>
> (p. 145)

Parsons suggests that although the obligations attached to *Gemeinschaft* are unspecified, they are in a certain sense still limited, but they are limited by an entirely different kind of limitation from that given in the *Gesellschaft* relation. The limitation of the obligations of *Gemeinschaft* derive from the fact that in this sphere, actors stand in a plurality of relations with others. The claims of the *Gemeinschaft* actor are therefore limited by the potentially conflicting claims of others.

Parsons argues, then, that the *Gemeinschaft* does contain a moral dimension, or value element, which is commonly held and *externally* enforceable. Yet in Weber's action typology, the communal orientation to action (*Vergemeinschaftung*) is based upon 'a subjective feeling of the parties, whether affectual or traditional, that they belong together' (Weber 1968: 40). Social relationships resting on value orientations are not part of *Gemeinschaft*, but are categorized as associative (*Vergesellschaftung*). According to Parsons (1973: 148), the moral element in Weber's scheme is therefore thrown over entirely to the category of 'legitimate order', where it is analysed within a means-end action scheme.

Thus, Weber's division of social relationships into communal and associative forms does not retain Tönnies' fundamental opposition between a body of actors unified through some form of objective necessity and an aggregate of individual actors, since the unity of the body of actors in *Gemeinschaft* does not simply lie in each individual's subjective experience of unity, but in objective conditions that lie outside the action of any single individual actor.

Moral attitudes

Working through the problems with Tönnies' dichotomous framework, it is possible to use the fundamental distinction he makes between two types of society, based on two types of social relationship, in conjunction with the idea that a different type of 'reason' might be involved in the structuring of communal forms of social organization. The reasoning behind action taking place in communal forms of social organization differs from that behind action in associative forms of organization in that the actors are not individuated; they are involved in relationships of interpersonal dependence. Their actions cannot be understood from the point of view of the autonomous subject.

Instead of using Tönnies' concept of an 'essential unity', with its connotations of absolute determinism, I use the notion of 'interpersonal dependence' to describe the ties that exist in communal forms of social organization. I refer to a relationship of interpersonal dependence existing between actors when objective conditions of dependence exist between actors who experience their relationship of dependence personally. In other words, a relationship of interpersonal dependence exists when actors are tied to particular others by material and/or normative conditions over which they have no direct control as an individual actor.

Because of these objective conditions, actors in a relationship of interpersonal dependence experience the overriding imperative to maintain their relationship. Like action in Tönnies' *Gemeinschaft*, the action involved between actors who are personally dependent upon another is an end in itself; it maintains the solidarity of the group. This means that in this action sphere the binding power of the norm, or its moral dimension, lies in the personal characteristics of actors acting in a concrete action context.

I use the notion of a moral attitude to depict the value orientation of actors in communal forms of social organization in order to highlight the extra-discursive dimension of morality here. Moral attitudes depict the orientation we take up when we relate to another. They can only be specified in a very broad way. Actor's must interpret each and every situation according to the particular context. Besides the broad, discursive content, moral attitudes also compromise interactive competences. We may wish 'to love and cherish' our spouse but putting this attitude into practice involves a degree of interpersonal skill.

Moreover, the obligations of actors in *Gemeinschaft* are not only defined by the broad, discursive content of norms, but are also defined in relation to the obligations of others in the group. These obligations are not decided once-and-for-all, but are continuously contested in a field of power relations, by the particular people involved who interpret the particular circumstances of each and every situation.[13]

The element of power involved needs to be analysed in relation to the conditions of social dependency that exist in the group. What needs to be considered is the individual's relation to the labour market, since this is the material basis of autonomy in capitalist societies, and the extent to which public services shift the burden of interpersonal forms of human dependence from women. I shall consider this question in more detail in the final chapter.

What needs to be considered at this point are concepts that might be useful for analysing the significance of different moral attitudes, as these reflect social relations that might be more or less oppressive to 'other'. I found it useful to differentiate two broad moral attitudes for this purpose, an attitude orientated towards understanding another and an attitude orientated towards coercing, or manipulating another.

Habermas' distinction between communicative and strategic action depends upon actors adopting one or other of these attitudes. Since his work elaborates the social relations that are associated with each attitude, I found his theory a useful starting point. However, it is necessary to first examine the way in which Habermas' central concepts occlude the moral dimension of communal forms of social organization.

Social relations and moral attitudes

Habermas' distinction between forms of rationality
Habermas distinguishes two forms of rationality which he associates with two forms of action, communicative and strategic. These forms of action are also associated with two organizing principles, or 'logics' which govern social life. Rather than identify communal and associative forms of social life, however, Habermas works with the notions of 'lifeworld' and 'system', concepts which ultimately allow him to bypass the need to deal with the conflicting claims to autonomy that characterize communal forms of social organization.

The advantage of Habermas' action scheme, though, is it allows us to see that a different form of rationality is possible. Reason no longer needs to be seen as purely instrumental/purposive. The communicative, or interpretive dimension of reason is highlighted which is based on an intersubjective social relation rather than a subject-object social relation.

Classical action theories contain only the possibility of subject-object social relations. Within these action schemes, the only relation that you and I can enter into is one of domination and submission. I can manipulate you or be manipulated by you; I can 'know' you or you can 'know' me. On the other hand, an intersubjective social relation is subject-subject. It introduces another way that I can relate to you. I can attempt to understand you and reach an agreement with you by way of negotiation and compromise.

What is important about Habermas' two forms of rationality, then, is their correspondence with two possible forms of social relation. The intersubjective social relation is associated with communicative action, the subject-object social relation is associated with strategic action, that is, instrumental/purposive action between two people (Habermas 1987: Introduction).

Habermas (1987: 86) argues that communicative action is a form of action because communicative acts 'take over the steering of social interactions'. That is, these acts of communication involve the participants in coordinating their future plans of action. Rather than future action plans being the outcome of one subject's attempts to manipulate the other, future action is arrived at through the mutual efforts of participants to reach a common understanding.

However, in co-opting Habermas' notion of the intersubjective social relation it is necessary to distance my use of the notion of an 'intersubjective social relation' from Habermas' concept of 'communicative action'. Communicative action as an action concept coordinates two perspectives through each participant adopting an orientation towards understanding, but Habermas avoids the need to explain why actors would adopt an understanding attitude. He does not conceptualize 'understanding' as a moral attitude, that needs to be analysed within a theory of power and inequality. Rather, he lifts out the notion of 'understanding' from Schutz's theory of the lifeworld and thereby avoids the whole question of how conflicting claims to autonomy are resolved in everyday life.

In Schutz's lifeworld, 'understanding' is the learning process whereby people acquire culture. People share common assumptions, which include common-sense notions of justice, in order to be able to interact at all in everyday life. We 'understand' each other simply by virtue of the fact that we have worldviews in common (Schutz 1970: 273). But why *should* I try and understand your perspective if it is different to mine and interferes with the pursuit of my own self-interest? Why should I subordinate my interests to yours if I am in a more powerful position than you? Schutz's lifeworld scheme gives us no way of analysing how different perspectives are coordinated when these different perspectives are in conflict.

Habermas' co-option of Schutz's notion of 'lifeworld' highlights the fundamental problem with Habermas' understanding of morality. Like Weber before him, the moral dimension of social life is reducible to the discursive content of norms, or codes of conduct that can be challenged by individuated actors. Yet in everyday life interaction, where norms are concretized, actors are not necessarily individuated. It is not just the terms of the contract, or language itself, that provides the cement for the social bond, or obligation, but relations of social dependence. This means that the legitimacy of an individual's claim is limited by the potentially conflicting claims of others. Whether actors resolve disputed claims through understanding and negotiation or coercion and manipulation depends upon the attitude they adopt.

While not wishing to elaborate further on Habermas' theory here,[14] suffice it say that his concept of communicative action cannot be used to analyse the moral dimension of communal forms of social organization because it assumes equality and individuation between all adult actors in everyday life. Communicative action may well be a useful concept for depicting the potential for *abstract* citizens, who are *formally* equal in the eyes of the law, to debate 'codes of conduct' in the public sphere, but it is unhelpful for considering the moral dimension of communal forms of social organization where adult actors are not individuated, at least equally.

Nevertheless, the notion of an 'intersubjective social relation' (S-S) as one which is formed through actors adopting an orientation towards trying to understand another can be contrasted with a subject-object social relation (S-O) where one actor attempts to impose his or her definition of a situation on another. It is a distinction which has the potential to describe different patterns of interaction as the outcome of different social relations. I use this distinction in the empirical study to describe two broad maternal attitudes.

'Maternal thinking' as a moral attitude

Sara Ruddick (1982: 77) opened up the possibility of a maternal logic in her influential essay, 'Maternal thinking'. Here she depicts mothering as a discipline involving judgements of success and failure. According to Ruddick, the intellectual activities involved in maternal thinking are 'distinguishable but not separable from disciplines of feeling'. Maternal thinking arises from maternal practices which dictate certain interests that guide the mother's judgements. These interests relate to the nurture and socialization of her child. Although the interest in nurture and socialization is universal, its forms are not. Ruddick's specific description of maternal thinking is based on her own experience with the institution of motherhood, in 'middle-class, white, Protestant, capitalist, patriarchal America' (p. 78).

While Ruddick's definition of maternal thinking has the advantage of linking, rather than separating, emotion, thought and judgement, her concept of maternal thought lacks any way of analysing this particular mode of thought as being socially constructed and socially constrained. I suggest that this problem would be overcome if the particular mode of maternal thought described by Ruddick was considered to be just one possible moral attitude adopted by mothers amongst any number of possibilities.

By referring to maternal thinking as a mode of thought, the concept can too easily be interpreted simply as a 'matter of taste', devoid of a moral element and subject to change through the action of individual mothers. In my view, the term can more usefully be used as a sociological concept if it is envisaged as a moral attitude. As a moral attitude it can be analysed as being socially constructed and socially sanctioned. The moral element becomes the central focus for sociological investigation, as does the particular socio-cultural environment which fosters this particular attitude in mothers.

As a moral attitude, its binding power could be investigated in terms of its location in a communal form of organization; in the action of particular mothers, caring for particular children in a particular socio-cultural environment. The binding power of maternal attitudes would be limited by the conflicting responsibilities of the mother, rather than the 'terms of the contract', or the validity claims inherent in speech acts. As women gain more autonomy and the opportunity to express their own interests, we could expect mothers to experience the conflict of interests between their own claim to autonomy and their child's more intensely, and bring idealized maternal attitudes into question.

The notion that maternal attitudes are contingent rather than essential, raises the question of how different maternal attitudes affect the nurturing process and the socialization of the child. Socialization theories draw on two major models of the self, George Herbert Mead's social learning theory and psychoanalytic accounts of the development of the self. In the next chapter, I discuss these models, and re-work some useful concepts to depict the constitution of the self as a relational process.

3 // The self in social theory

Feminists have challenged psychological models of child development for their failure to locate the mother as a separate individual and for their inability to accommodate the diversity of child-rearing practices that exist, even in Western societies. However, this challenge does not contribute towards the development of an alternative model of child development, orientated towards a feminist value system, grounded in an ethics of care and concern for others. What is missing is a way of conceptualizing the constitution of a self that is autonomous, yet which is also capable of recognizing and accommodating the claim to autonomy of others. What is needed is a relational account of the constitution of the self, an account which recognizes that autonomy must be actively constructed by an (m)other, in a particular socio-cultural context that values the objective of autonomy and enhances the (m)other's own claim to autonomy.

Rather than reject psychological theories of the self outright, I propose to work through the basic assumptions on which these theories have been built and expose the ways in which they occlude the subjectivity of the (m)other and the particular socio-cultural context in which she performs nurturing activity. In this way, I hope to set out some useful concepts for situating a psychological model of the constitution of the self within a feminist value system.

Social theory relies on two broadly defined traditions for understanding the constitution of the self, social learning theory, derived from the social psychology of George Herbert Mead, and psychoanalytic theory. These two traditions have very different conceptions about the nature of the 'self'. For Mead and his followers, the self is primarily a cognitive structure, derived from the institutionalized patterns of behaviour that the individual has in common with another. On the other hand, the psychoanalytic 'self' is primarily an embodied, or physiological structure, grounded in one person's recognition of what is particular about another.

While both these traditions have useful concepts that help illuminate the nature of the 'self', neither tradition offers us a truly relational conception of the constitution of the self, that might help us understand the significance of the subjectivity of the (m)other. Central concepts, then, need to be examined more closely to see how they obscure the perspective of the (m)other and her active contribution to the construction of the culture's value systems. They then need to be reconsidered with the intersubjective perspective, developed in the last chapter, in mind. I shall consider some useful concepts from G.H. Mead's social psychology, then explore some important themes from psychoanalysis.

G.H. Mead's 'social' self

Mead's (1962) account of socialization is grounded in a notion of the self that is connected to other selves through the internalization of institutionalized behaviour patterns, or social 'roles'. Social roles are constructed in a complementary fashion, reflecting the reciprocal expectations we have of the behaviour of others. The child appropriates these roles through a learning process, depicted by Mead in terms of 'Taking the attitude of the other'. Before discussing Mead's process of socialization in more detail, it is necessary for the reader to grasp how Mead understands the concept of 'meaning', since it is at this most fundamental level that the socially contingent nature of nurturing is occluded.

Mead sees cultural 'meanings' as being derived from nature, from the functional requirements of bodily needs. Meanings are not, in themselves, cultural products. It is the expression of the meaning that is culturally defined:

> Nature has meaning and implication but not indication by symbols. The symbol is distinguishable from the meaning it refers to. Meanings are in nature, but symbols are the heritage of man.
>
> (1962: 180, n. 26)

The assumption here is that meanings have an objective reality that can be 'known', directly, by another who grasps the functional intention of the act. It is not the 'knowing' process that is a cultural product, but the symbolization that is given to the meaning.

This assumption that the body has pre-given 'needs', or requirements that can be functionally specified and known directly by another is a common assumption in the literature on child-rearing across all disciplines. It is directly associated with a dichotomous formulation of mind and body and the idea that the body has a fixed, universal form. What, then, are the implications of Mead's understanding of 'meaning' for our attempts to locate the (m)other's contribution to the socialization process?

If meanings are given as an objective reality in the social act between two parties, we must assume that the child's gestures have an inbuilt intention, namely to 'express' his or her 'instincts' or bodily 'needs'. The child 'knows' what it wants and attempts to indicate what it wants to the mother, who either identifies the correct meaning of the child's actions or she does not. In this scenario, in order to 'know' her child's needs, the (m)other does not appear to be involved in a social activity with any one else but her child. Her interpretive activity is limited to correctly identifying the 'right' meaning. The so-called 'social' act between the (m)other and child is purely instrumental, operating in a stimulus-response mode.

Thus, if we were to rely on Mead's conception of meaning, a strategic action scheme would appear to be sufficient to analyse maternal-infant interaction and there would be no need to locate the (m)other's perspective since the particularities of the (m)other and the child make no difference to the outcome. She either correctly identifies the meaning and makes the culturally approved response, or she does not.

In Mead's account of socialization, the actual socializing mechanism is a learning process which he calls 'taking the attitude of the other'. Successful nurturing lays the foundation for this process by providing the child with the concrete emotional experiences and ties of attachment to particular others. But these emotional exchanges operate in a simplistic stimulus-response mode, where the actual emotions that are exchanged between parent and child, love and anger, are assumed to be 'natural'. It is during the next phase of the child's development that the emotions become socialized, when the child learns to generalize his or her responses to all others in the community.

Taking the attitude of the other
Mead describes this process as occurring in two stages. In the first stage, the child takes over the expectations of particular others in specific situations. These expected responses, or patterned ways of behaving, are the 'attitudes' of others. These attitudes then become the basic building blocks for the child's internalized social world.

Mead (1962: 230) draws an analogy with the distinction between 'play' and 'game' in order to depict the difference between the early phase of taking the attitude of the other and the next phase in which the child learns to generalize his or her responses to include the social expectations of all others in the community. During play, the child utilizes his or her own responses to stimuli in a way that reflects the child's perception of the particular people about him or her. Children play at being others by adopting the characteristics of those they know.

During the next phase, the 'game', the child must be able to assume the role of all others involved in the game. The child must know the rules of the game, that represent the common attitude of the group, or 'the generalized other'. In adopting the attitude of the 'generalized other' the child takes on the attitudes of the organized social group to which he or she belongs towards the organized, cooperative social activity of that group. These organized social attitudes are called 'roles', which are constructed in a complementary and mutually satisfying manner.[1]

One great weakness in Mead's account of socialization is that it underplays the role of conflict. The self consists of organized roles, constituted in a complementary fashion. Mead's self is a social self, a self that reflects what one individual has in common with another (p. 239). He does emphasize the importance of individuation, or autonomy, but this is simply a developmental stage, a cognitive achievement.

He uses a distinction between 'I' and 'ME' to illuminate the individuated dimension of the self. The 'ME' is the perspective of the self that houses the expectations of the generalized other. It is that part of ourselves that directly reflects social roles, or institutionalized ways of behaving. The 'I' is that part of the self which responds to the attitudes of others. It becomes aware of the socially organized 'ME', but although significantly influenced by its perception of 'ME', the 'I' does not always act in accordance with the 'ME'. There is an element of uncertainty and spontaneity in the 'I' which allows for novel experience, making action less predictable and allowing for the possibility of change (pp. 242–7).

Thus, in Mead's account, individuation is achieved simply through the child reaching a developmental stage. It is the *cognitive* capacity of humans that allows for individuality. Individuation requires only the ability to be self-reflexive. This can be achieved developmentally. It is not envisaged as a form of subjectivity comprising certain emotional, or psychological complexes. As we shall now see, this account differs fundamentally from the psychoanalytic self.

Psychoanalysis and the embodied self

The essential difference between Mead's conception of self and the psychoanalytic notion of self is that the fundamental building blocks of the psychoanalytic self are the child's own particular instinctual drives. Moreover, psychoanalytic theory provides us with the insight that the body is not just an object, worked on by wider social processes and cognition. The body is active in moral development; it plays a significant role in the structuring of the mind, or psyche.

This is because psychoanalysis conceives of the individual fundamentally in terms of the body's basic 'drives' or 'instincts'. One individual's set of drives is essentially *antagonistic* to all others. The psychoanalytic Ego is built up as a result of this conflict. The agency of the child, or the role of the 'irrational' or 'unconscious' dimension of human interaction,

is structured into the child's psyche. Thus, the patterning of 'inner nature' is derived from the essential conflict between one particular self
and all others, rather than from the assimilation of a pre-existing social
harmony through a learning process.[2]

Thus, psychoanalytic theory helps to illuminate the role of the body
in the constitution of social ties. Unlike the 'social' self depicted by
Mead, which consists of commonly shared symbols, the psychoanalytic
Ego is derived from the inevitable conflict between one particular individual and all other individuals. The origins of this conflict lie in the
fundamental antagonism that exists between one particular individual's
bodily drives and the social environment in which these drives are
expressed. The Ego is formed as a result of this conflict.

Mothering in Freud's account of psychic development

The cornerstone of Freud's theory of human motivation is the Pleasure
Principle. Freud (1950: 43; 1962: 30; 1976: 401–3) believed that man[3]
was motivated by the tensions created in the two sets of instincts he
housed; Eros, the life-preserving instincts which include the sexual instinct and Thantos, the instincts incorporating destruction and aggression which lead the individual towards death. These two sets of instincts
set up excitations which must be satisfied. Their gratification is accompanied by the physical sensations of pleasure and pain which motivate
the organism to act in accordance with the principle of 'achieving pleasure and avoiding unpleasure' (1976: 401).[4]

In order to seek pleasure and avoid pain, the organism must ensure
that Eros is gratified, but the instincts which comprise Eros are brought
into conflict when confronted by the social world. Satisfying the sexual
instinct is often not in the interests of the instinct for self-preservation.
A tension is set up between these instincts. The organism's way of
dealing with this tension is to 'split' the psyche into component parts
(1950: 5–6).

The differentiation of the psyche into the first two component parts,
the Ego and the Id is the organism's way of dealing with the tensions
in his instincts that occur as he confronts obstacles in the external world.
It is a reactive phenomenon. The psyche is then able to cope with this
tension either by repressing in the unconscious Id those instinctual
expressions which are likely to be met with hostility in the external
world, or by modifying their expression into socially acceptable forms.
This task is taken on by the Ego, which has the function of substituting
the Reality Principle for the Pleasure Principle. The substitution is itself
painful, but the painful experiences can also be repressed in the unconscious (Freud 1950: 5–6).

In this early phase of development, the mother is the external reality
confronted by the child. She acts either as the source of the infant's
gratification, or as the source of the infant's frustration. In either case,
the difference that the mother makes is not relevant to the development

of the child's value systems, since her actions merely induce feelings of satisfaction or frustration, pain or pleasure. At this pre-oedipal stage of development, the child does not associate its actions with 'good' or 'bad' but with satisfaction or frustration.

When performing nurturing activity, the mother is seen here as a vehicle, both for nature and culture. She is a means to an end. She gratifies the pre-existing, instinctual impulses of the child and acts to constrain them within the pre-existing, socially approved forms. It is not possible to conceive of her as a subject while nurturing, actively constructing cultural value systems. The mother represents an external reality to which neither she nor her child contributes, at least while nurturing.

The external reality to which both the mother and child must conform is created somewhere outside their sphere of interaction. The values and ideals which structure this external reality are internalized by the child after a further split in the psyche has occurred and the Super Ego is created. The role of the father and the oedipus struggle is central here.

The oedipus situation (Freud 1962: 21–3) arises when the child wishes to achieve sexual satisfaction with his first love-object, the mother. This wish appears to be blocked by the father. The child experiences feelings of intense hostility towards the father, but he loves the father too. In this ambiguity lies the first stirring of moral guilt, induced by the child's fear that his aggression will obliterate the one who is also loved. Moral guilt is therefore seen to have its origins in an ambiguous and intense emotional experience. It is an experience which results in a tension within the child's own contradictory instincts.

The solution to this dilemma brought about during the oedipus confrontation is for the child to identify with the father's ideals, that is, with the obstacles inhibiting the fulfilment of the wish. This is done by erecting the same obstacles within the psychic apparatus. The obstacles in the path of the child's wish fulfilment become internalized as ideals, splitting the Ego into another compartment, the Super Ego, consisting of the Ego-ideal and the conscience. The Super Ego tells the child how he or she should behave. Its strength depends upon the authoritative power of the father. The more powerful the father figure, the greater the domination of the Super Ego over the Id (Freud 1962: 24–5).

The problem of connectedness

Included in this account of the development of the human psyche, is the premise that the psyche begins its life in a holistic state, from which it splits as a result of conflict. According to this premise, the infant begins life in a state of 'connectedness', or a feeling of oneness with the external environment, represented by the mother. Freud (1953: 92) referred to this period of the infant's life as the period of absolute, or primary narcissism, during which phase the infant's needs could be directly gratified.[5]

Freud regarded this state of 'connectedness' as naturally occurring, giving the infant much pleasure. He believed that the feeling of connectedness acted as something of a lure, beckoning men back to a state which Freud's linear conception of development envisaged as regressive. Furthermore, since the mother is the infant's 'external environment' associated with this feeling of connectedness, women are regarded as a regressive influence, opposed to civilization because they are unable to complete development as separate individuals. They remain representatives of family and sexual life, where they soon 'come into opposition with civilization' and display their 'retarding and restraining influence' (p. 40).

In my view, it is the theory of narcissism that obscures the mother's contribution to the moral development of the child. This theory rests on the premise that the infant's instincts can be directly 'known' and therefore directly satisfied (or frustrated). What it overlooks is the fact that instincts must be interpreted as needs by another, prior to there being any experience of satisfaction or frustration on the part of the infant.

If we reject the assumption that the child begins life in a state of fusion with the mother,[6] the notion of connectedness becomes problematic. The question that comes into focus is *how* connectedness is achieved by the mother. How does she come to 'know' what the instinctual impulses of the child mean? Freudian drive theory, like Mead's social learning theory, begins from the premise that the child's instinctual impulses have a functionally specified goal. The period of primary narcissism is that period when these goals can be directly gratified (or frustrated). Once again, it does not appear that the mother's actions here make any difference other than in the sense of giving the child the optimal level of frustration to allow for the splitting of the psyche and the development of the Ego.

If we consider that connectedness is itself problematic, that is, as depending upon a social process, then the way in which the mother comes to 'know' the needs of her child might make some conceivable difference to the moral development of the child. In other words, it becomes possible to imagine that different forms of connectedness might exist. Connectedness, as described by Freud (1973: 6) is an absolute term. It remains unaffected by the structuring of the psyche and plays no active part in its development. It is simply preserved intact, as a 'primitive' aspect of the mind.[7]

The first problem that needs addressing in reinterpreting the problem of connectedness is Freud's theory of human motivation which rests on the premise that the individual is primarily motivated by the desire to experience pleasure and avoid pain. This theory of human motivation cannot be re-interpreted within an intersubjective perspective, because the individual infant's impulses are understood only from the perspective of the isolated, individual child. So long as we view human motivation in this way, we must understand socialization as fundamentally a process of repression and individual adaption to social norms. Object-relations theory has some important insights to offer us here. In particular, object-relations theorists question the primacy given to drive theory. They also introduce the idea that the child is fundamentally social, in that the child's primary goal is not to reduce tension, but to maintain a 'good' caring relationship.

Mothering in object-relations theory

Analysing human relationships from the perspective of the individual organism is a fundamental deficiency in Freud's theory of human motivation which has been addressed by psychoanalysts in the object-relations tradition. Beginning with the work of Melanie Klein[8] and her theory of internalized object relationships, writers in this tradition have developed an alternative to the Pleasure Principle to explain the basis of human motivation. There is a general agreement amongst these writers that the infant is not primarily motivated by the desire to seek pleasure and avoid pain, but by the more fundamental need to sustain the parental relationship itself.

Within this tradition, the child's actions only become meaningful if we consider them in relation to the child's primary need to secure a 'good' object relationship. 'Good' and 'bad' inner objects are highly exaggerated and fantasized representations of the real relationships that the child experiences. These good and bad objects are not just internalized during the oedipus confrontation but are internalized from the very beginning of the infant's exposure to the external world.

According to Hanna Segal's (1979: 114) interpretation of Klein's work, the crucial difference with Freud's account of psychic development is that Klein claims that the infant is able to experience anxiety from birth whereas Freud believed the oedipus struggle marked the beginning of the child's experience of anxiety. Since the child can experience anxiety from birth, they must also build up defences against this anxiety during the first few years of life. These defences would be derived from the child's earliest emotional experiences with the mother.

If the child is able to experience intense emotional ambiguities *before* the oedipal phase, then the mother's contribution to moral development is made significant and the question arises as to whether the experience of conflict with the mother is a qualitatively different type of experience than conflict with the father.

According to Segal (1979: 81), Klein conceives of two different types of moral guilt, 'reparative' guilt, which has its origins in the child's early relational experiences with the mother and 'repressive' guilt which refers to the moral guilt induced as a result of the oedipal confrontation with the father. Children have the potential to experience reparative guilt when they can no longer 'split' the 'good' and 'bad' aspects of their experiences with their mother. Thus, the good and bad experiences with their mother can no longer be internalized separately. This marks the 'depressive' position, when the infant experiences the mother as a whole person and can no longer keep the 'good' and the 'bad' experiences of her separate. In a process analogous to Freud's oedipus situation, the child experiences an emotional ambiguity: the mother is both the source of the child's gratification and the object of the child's aggression.

The fear of the mother's loss is intensely felt by the child who still feels insecure with regard to maintaining a good inner object-relation. The child feels that this loss is due to his or her own feelings of hostility and this leads to the development of a new emotional complex, reparative guilt. The basis of reparative guilt is formed as the infant attempts to resolve the dilemma by making restitution to the mother. It is this restitutive idea, the idea that the experience of grief will lead the child towards the desire to try to heal the mother, that is the basis of reparative guilt and it is here that Klein locates the origins of the child's feelings of concern for another. If not experienced by the child before the depressive position has been fully developed, the child will develop new defences against experiencing this pain, the symptoms of which are remarkably similar to the narcissistic individual of contemporary social theorizing.

Klein then describes a range of restitutive and reparative mechanisms that children develop in order to restore their good object, that is to heal their relationship with their mother, but according to Segal's (1979: 81–2) account of this position, the 'reappearance of his mother and her care for him are essential to this process'. This insight into the emotional exchange that takes place between the mother and the child requires far more development, but this development is hindered even within this tradition, because of the inability to locate the mother's subjectivity in these crucial emotional exchanges.

Followers of Klein have not developed the implications of the concept of reparative guilt with respect to Freud's theory of narcissism and the essential nature 'connectedness'. There still exists the tendency to rely on the fundamental assumptions contained in Freudian drive theory to explain human motivation. According to Harry Guntrip (1969: 204), in the Kleinian model the hostility of the child is still seen as part of the essential conflict between the child's own instincts rather than as part of an emotional exchange with the mother. By relying on Freud's instinct, or drive theory the problem of the mother's subjectivity and how this relates to the emotional exchange implied by the concept of reparative guilt cannot be analysed.

This means that once again, the mother's actions are considered to have only instrumental meaning. She either frustrates the child's instinctual demands or she satisfies them. Her actions are not considered to take their meaning from part of a larger community of actors. This is because, once again, the infant's 'needs' do not appear to require interpretation. Fusion, from the mother's perspective, does not have to be actively brought about through interpretive activity. The infant's 'needs' appear as self-evident, an objective reality outside the mother's efforts to understand them, or structure them as 'needs'. Thus, rather than becoming structured during the activity which results in connectedness, the theory of object-relations only considers how drives come to be structured as a result of the satisfaction or frustration of drives. Even though object-relations theory has opened up the way to analysing the mother's contribution to the structuring of the child's self, the belief persists that the child's bodily needs can be known directly. A 'good-enough mother' will know what her child needs and satisfy these appropriately. The inner structuring of the child occurs only through conflict situations, in the interplay of satisfaction and frustration. We still do not know how the structuring of the child's inner world might be affected by the interpretive activity that is carried out by the mother.

Although object-relations writers open up the possibility that the mother's actions do make a difference, her actions can only be envisaged as making an instrumental difference. Thus, the potential for cultural differences to occur in the structuring of the self, as a result of the mother's interpretive activity, cannot be explored.

Instead, since the potential of the mother to 'know' her child's 'needs' is taken for granted by psychoanalytic theorists, writers in the object-relations school believe that the mother's contribution to her child's autonomy lies in minimizing the child's negative emotional experiences. Thus, there exists the belief that it is possible for the mother to create a near-perfect care-giving environment, in which the child's experience of 'bad' object relations would be minimal. Followers of the object-relations tradition tend to advocate such an ideal setting, which would be catered for by a mother well attuned to her child.[9]

Self psychology: individuation as parental recognition

The attempt by object-relations writers to turn Freud's intrapsychic model into a relational perspective has been hampered by the lack of a clearly defined concept of the subject, or self. Self psychology has attempted to fill this gap. There are a number of positions which have been put forward to elaborate on the concept of the self. Heinz Kohut's contribution to this branch of psychoanalysis, known as self psychology is useful because of his attempt to locate the parenting perspective in the developmental process. Kohut's work is also important because feminist writers such as Jessica Benjamin are beginning to utilize some of his central concepts.[10]

Kohut (1983: ch. 4) describes the self as being constituted during interaction with an empathetic, or responsive parent. It has two poles in a tension that promotes action. The first pole is 'ambition', secured with the child's affective experience of parental recognition. This pole is made possible by an empathetic parent who merges affectively with the child and responds in a way that confirms the child's 'self-assertive presence' (p. 171).

In order for this first pole to be secured, the child must experience being idealized by a loving parent who is affected by the child and responds appropriately to the child's needs, allowing the child to exhibit a degree of omnipotence, and 'healthy exhibitionism' (p. 171). Thus, the development of an independent self requires confirmation of autonomy from another. This 'other' is a particular other, who idealizes the child and is affected by the child. Being affected by the child, the empathetic parent will recognize this particular child and confirm the child's still vulnerable 'creative-productive-active self' (p. 76).

The second pole is that of 'ideals', constituted by the idealizing activity of the child who admires the parent. The parent is now recognized and idealized by the child as someone worthy of emulation. This pole provides the child with the ideals that guide future action. The first pole, ambition, drives the self while the second, that of ideals, leads the self. Together, these two poles form the 'nuclear self', a structure which 'is the basis for our sense of being an independent centre of initiative and perception' (p. 177).

Kohut suggests that the early constituents of the self, that are secured through parental recognition, are predominantly derived from maternal-infant interaction: 'the mother's mirroring acceptance confirms nuclear grandiosity; her holding and carrying allows merger experiences with the self-object's idealized omnipotence' (p. 179). However, the components of the latter pole, that of ideals, may come from parental figures of either sex.

Unlike drive theory, Kohut's self psychology is able to focus on the influence of the external environment and the real relationships of the child in the active production of the autonomous self. This shift in focus allows us to locate the centrality of the actions of the parent in producing the autonomous self, but how does Kohut's theory of the constitution of the self relate to the insights provided by object-relations theory?

Kohut believes that his self psychology is simply complementary to Freudian drive theory. His intention is to clarify the pathology of narcissistic disorders which, he says, are derived from unempathetic parenting. However, he believes that drive psychology is still necessary to analyse patients who have had 'grossly unempathetic parenting' (p. 77). Kohut does not attempt to integrate these two paradigms because he believes that they may more fruitfully be utilized as two complementary theoretical frameworks.

Kohut's interpretation of drive theory is rather different, however, to classical psychoanalysis. In Kohut's view, socialization is more or less enriching, rather than more or less repressive, depending upon the quality of parenting. For example, in discussing aggression, Kohut is emphatic that rage and destructiveness should not be envisaged as an 'instinct' searching for an outlet, but as part of a pattern, or network of responses that have been built up as regressive products, 'as fragments of the broader psychological configurations that make up the nuclear self' (p. 118). If the child receives empathetic parenting, aggression will become part of the psychological configurations that make up the self-assertive, nuclear self. Rage and destructiveness are the product of the aggressive instincts failing to become established as self-assertiveness, through empathetic parenting.

On the other hand, however, Kohut falls back into classic drive theory when he attempts to explain a parent's 'over-indulgence'. In describing the case history of one of his narcissistic patients, Kohut (p. 78) informs us that some extremely empathetic and devoted mothers may be seen to be depriving the child 'of the opportunity for building psychic structure . . . in consequence of the non-frustration of drives the Ego remains immature . . .'. He is supporting here the ideal of 'optimal frustration', that is, the child-rearing principle that some limits have to be set on drives if the psychic structure is to differentiate and become enriched.

However, in the example he describes, Kohut remarks that over-indulgence does not appear to be the problem. The problem is that the mother and grandmother of the patient are unable to distinguish their own drives from that of the child. It is their own drives they are indulging and not the child's. How, then, do adequate parents come to distinguish two sets of drives, and how are these two sets of drives reconciled?

There must surely be some fundamental emotional conflict here, similar perhaps to Klein's account of the experience of reparative guilt. If conflict remains a central consideration, how does this conflict relate to the experience of affective merging? Kohut avoids these questions by using the concept of empathy in very much the same way as object-relations writers resort to the concept of maternal instinct.

Empathy as an intersubjective action sequence

In Kohut's work, empathy has a 'mirroring' function. It is the mechanism through which the child's developing sense of self is recognized and confirmed. Kohut also uses empathy as a regulatory device, in that it is also the mechanism which allows the parent to evaluate what might constitute 'over-indulgence'. But empathy does not appear as part of an interpretive process. It has the function of unifying the child's self, rather than the perspectives of the parent and child.

As the child's 'mirror', empathy refers only to the moment of affective merger between the parent and child; a temporary fusion, or feeling of connectedness during which the parent becomes aware of the child's needs. The merger itself, however, is taken for granted by Kohut. He does not question how this occurs, except to say that the bulk of this merging is done by the 'maternal self-object' while holding and carrying the infant (p. 179). Merging appears as a static moment of affective comprehension, induced in the parent through the transmission of the child's affective signals.

If, on the other hand, empathy was envisaged as the outcome of an interpretive process, it would have to be achieved and the way in which it was achieved would be brought into focus. A number of recent papers on empathy suggest that empathy has a rational as well as an affective dimension. These papers suggest the necessity of understanding the overall process which results in an affective merger.

For example, both Buie (1981) and Basch (1983) observe that empathy is a dynamic process of making inferences. Buie (1981: 293) argues that we do not know directly what another is feeling. We make inferences which are based on our own experience. We compare the cues that are being transmitted with our own inner resources, built up as a result of our own object-relations.

Basch (1983: 110–11) also argues for a dynamic concept of empathy as 'finding' or 'searching' one's way into the experience of another. He defines empathy as:

> a hermeneutic circle in which resonance, interpretation, and evaluation all play an essential part. An affective experience of one's own is first identified as a response to or resonance with another; this leads to a reasoned, though not necessarily conscious, interpretation of what this means or says about the other; this postulated conclusion about the other's mental state is then subjected to validation or disconfirmation by testing it against reality through further reflection, observation, or experiment.
>
> (p. 111)

It would seem fruitful, then, to use the concept of empathy as the moment of fusion when a common understanding has been reached about the meaning of the infant's actions. Basch's definition highlights the importance of both the affective and cognitive elements which lead up to this merger and the ongoing, evaluative dimension, whereby the definition of the situation is assessed and reassessed.[11]

As an hermeneutic experience, the achievement of maternal, empathetic understanding has the potential to be investigated within an intersubjective action scheme in which the interaction between two subjects can be analysed. The concept of an intersubjective social relation (S-S) may be fruitfully used here, so long as the affective and embodied aspect of empathetic understanding is kept in mind. In addition, instead of two communicatively competent subjects in interaction, maternal empathetic understanding would involve the mother in constructing the perspective of the child. Since the mother must take the actions of the child into account when constructing this perspective, both the mother and child can still be considered agents.

An intersubjective action scheme has the advantage of bringing the process of action coordination into focus. It allows us to analyse the way in which two separate perspectives are coordinated. This process of coordination must inevitably involve the mother and child in conflict as well as merger. Classical drive theory assumes the state of merger and focuses on conflict. Self psychology focuses on the merger and cannot accommodate conflict. However, the use of an intersubjective action scheme has the advantage of illuminating the relationship between these two dimensions of maternal-infant interaction.

Although both Jessica Benjamin and Nancy Chodorow have coopted Habermas' notion of an intersubjective social relation to locate the (m)other as a separate subject, they have not retained the Habermas' intention to use the concept as an interpretive mechanism. By using the notion of an intersubjective social relation to depict the interpretive efforts of the mother to 'know' the needs of the child, the concept can more fruitfully be used to focus on the question of how the perspectives of the (m)other and the child are coordinated.

Unlike Habermas' concept of communicative action, empathetic understanding must accommodate the role of conflict and the body in the interpretive activity carried out by the (m)other. The role of the body in the interpretive action of the (m)other–infant dyad is crucial. When the (m)other attempts to understand from the child's point of view, something actually happens to both the (m)other and the child. It is not just that the (m)other has worked something out in her mind. She has an important affective experience, as does the child when the (m)other acts on this sensation. This means that it is just as important to investigate what happens to the (m)other while nurturing as it is to investigate what happens to the child, since the affective sensations experienced by the (m)other while nurturing structure future patterns of interaction.

An intersubjective action scheme analysing the mother–infant dyad needs to be able to depict empathetic understanding as an embodied experience for both parties involved. It must also be able to accommodate both the moments of 'misunderstanding', or conflict, as well as the moments of merger, since it is these affective experiences of merger and conflict which constitute the child's subjectivity.

These last two chapters have been intended to provide conceptual tools to help locate the mother as a subject while nurturing. I now turn to the ethnographic study to provide a concrete, descriptive account of nurturing activity.

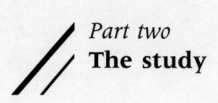

Part two
The study

4 // The study

Playgroups: history and general characteristics

The study begins from the premise that an infant's needs cannot be known objectively. Nurturing activity must therefore consist of interpretive acts, which refer and feed into a particular socio-cultural milieu, as well as the caring activity that is defined as necessary by these interpretive acts. In adopting a method to understand the dynamics of the interpretive process involved in nurturing activity, it was therefore necessary to consider a venue where the dyad could be observed in a particular socio-cultural environment. Most studies of maternal-infant interaction have focused almost exclusively on the dyad, isolated from any particular socio-cultural milieu, and observed in the home or a laboratory setting.[1]

The informal friendship networks of mothers seemed an appropriate place to observe the interaction of the dyad within a particular socio-cultural setting. Studies by Richards (1983) and Wearing (1984) have shown that mothers participate in frequent formal and informal meetings with kin, neighbours and other mothers. One such meeting place which provides ready access to a participant observer is the playgroup.

Playgroups are regular, social get-togethers of mothers and carers and their children. They are often initiated by mothers as a way of overcoming what they see as inadequate opportunities for socializing in their neighbourhoods. They first made their appearance in New Zealand in 1941 as an outcome of educational policy, designed to promote the involvement of parents in children's play and the parents' awareness of the importance of play as an early educational experience.[2] The idea was promoted among pre-school educational groups and playgroups began to appear in Britain in the early 1960s. In Britain, as in New Zealand, playgroups are most often initiated by paid facilitators and their play activities structured by paid play leaders, funded by parent contributions. Like its counterpart in New Zealand, the British Playgroup Association has a public voice, which in Britain has been associated with parents' demands for greater public involvement in nursery education and public criticism of the lack of social planning for children.

The playgroup movement made its first appearance in Australia in the early 1970s and expanded very rapidly. It differs from the New Zealand and British experience in that the organization of groups has been left far more to the parents themselves, rather than being placed in the hands of paid play leaders and facilitators. The Australian Pre-school Playgroup Association has also been vocal in its public criticism of the lack of social planning for children, and in 1975 it received its first official funding from the Federal Government to provide support and advice to community and novice groups. Other services provided by the Playgroup Association include information services, field workers and toy and book libraries.

Today there are a vast array of parents' and carers' groups calling themselves playgroups. Many just comprise friends, who come together in one another's homes at a regular time each week. Others meet in local halls, community centres and parks and may or may not be affiliated with the central Playgroup Association. Their popularity reflects certain needs perceived by mothers and carers of children under school age. These include:

1 The need to create opportunities for informal socializing among preschool age children in their own neighbourhoods.
2 The need to meet and talk with other parents and carers about their child-rearing experiences.

In the Hunter Region of New South Wales, Australia, where the study was carried out, there are a small number of playgroups that receive input from government funded child-care workers. However, the vast majority of playgroups still rely heavily on the organization of the parents and carers themselves. It is state government policy to leave as much of the organizing and supervision of playgroups to parents. Government assistance is only forthcoming if playgroups are linked to family support programmes which offer special assistance to families targeted by Department of Community Services' (DOCS)[3] workers as 'at risk'.

Mothers and other adults caring for young children seek out playgroups that are convenient, in terms of locality and time, and that are amenable, in terms of the personalities of the other members of the group. They differ widely in this respect. Each group comes to reflect the norms of its regular attenders and may vary with time as the regulars move out of the group and new members take their place.

Carers may attend once or twice and decide that the group is not to their liking. They may then seek out another group that is more in tune with their own values and normative expectations. There is, then, an element of voluntarism in the carer's choice of a group, but this is limited by such factors as the carer's access to transport and the accessibility of other groups in the area.

Having been involved in a number of playgroups when my own children were young,[4] I knew that playgroups differed considerably in the way they were organized. I also knew that the norms guiding the interaction of group members differed considerably depending upon who was attending the group. By joining in with their activities, I hoped to be able to observe and describe the dynamics of the group. I was particularly interested in the way in which the need to maintain friendship links with other group members, influenced interaction within the dyad.

I also assumed that it would be less constraining on the natural flow of the dyad's interaction if I observed the dyad in a playgroup setting rather than in individual homes. I felt that mothers would be less influenced by the presence of an observer in a group situation, since the observer's focus would not fall constantly on any single individual mother.

The playgroup venues

I began the study by attending a playgroup venue that operated three mornings a week from a Family Support Service, in a community cottage located at Westville[5] in the western suburbs of Newcastle, New South Wales. As the study progressed, I decided to attend two other playgroup venues, in order to gauge whether the patterns of interaction I was observing in Westville were also typical of other playgroups. I thought that different groups might bring out different patterns that would highlight areas requiring more intensive study. Any contrasting patterns would have to be explained and this would enable me to build up and expand my theoretical model.

I chose the next two venues with a view to including as much demographic diversity as possible given the constraints on my time and mobility. This procedure is in accord with Glaser and Strauss' (1970) model of 'Theoretical sampling', a process of data collection for generating theory. According to Glaser and Strauss (p. 107), the adequate theoretical sample is judged on the basis of how widely and diversely analysts choose their groups for 'saturating categories' as they emerge from analysis.

I have characterized the three playgroup venues with general demographic data, derived from the 1986 census and the basic demographic data that I gathered from the more regular attenders.

1 *The 'suburban' playgroup*
The 'suburban' playgroup operated three mornings a week from a family support service in Westville, in Newcastle's western suburbs. The

Westville area itself is made up of an older, small town surrounded by new housing estates which have attracted a large number of families with young children. The area surrounding the playgroup venue is densely populated with young families of diverse life experience. It provided a potentially rich site for observing group dynamics and interactive patterns because of the diversity of life experience that carers brought with them to the larger group.

This venue had provided carers in the past with the services of a play leader, but the play leader had recently been withdrawn following new state government recommendations that the play leader only be used for families targeted as 'at risk'. Nevertheless, many of the mothers and other carers who attended this venue, did so because its organization required less commitment on their behalf than smaller groups meeting in private homes.

The suburban venue was attended by large numbers of carers and children. There was always a sufficient number of volunteers to organize activities, so that carers did not feel obligated to attend regularly and contribute to the group's organization. This was convenient for the mothers who worked part time, particularly those who were called in to work at short notice and could not give the commitment necessary to be a volunteer organizer.

The most striking aspect about this venue, then, was the large number of carers and children who attended and the extent of the localities from which they were drawn. Numbers at each playgroup meeting averaged 15 carers and 17 children, although there were times when over 25 carers attended and about 30 children. As in the other groups I observed, very few, if any, attended on rainy days and the numbers dropped considerably during the school holidays.

Although there always appeared to be a regular core of about 7–10 carers attending on a particular week day, there were many more who appeared irregularly, fitting playgroup in with their paid work commitments. Some of these brought their friends or relatives with them when they came, others met with one or two of the carers there and formed their own smaller group within the larger group. A few carers never attempted to get to know other carers, but used the play facilities to spend time enjoying an outing with their child. As one mother put it, this playgroup venue was more like 'a pre-school environment' for the children in that only the core group of regulars really got to know each other well.

The high numbers of participants at this venue had the disadvantage of making it extremely difficult to get to know well all those present. It was often confusing having so many coming and going, since I never knew if the carer I was observing one week would come back again. However, I did get to know most of the regular attenders and their general patterns of interaction with their children and each other. In addition, there were usually one or two carers whose interactive patterns provided a contrast with the others present.

Organization of the suburban group

Playgroup operated from the suburban venue three mornings a week. Each of these three groups had their own playgroup committee of volunteer carers who met once a month to decide on the general running of the playgroup and the jobs that needed to be done. Tasks were allocated to volunteers on a roster basis, and included setting up different play activities, cutting up fruit for the children and cleaning up. The committees also organized fund raising events and the occasional weekend picnic to include fathers.

The influence of the professional child-care worker who helped to set up the suburban playgroups in the past could still be seen in the organization of the play area, in that the play environment at this venue was set up each morning to include carers in the activities of their children as much as possible. Encouraging parental involvement in play is a stated aim of the Children's Services division of DOCS from which the group obtains funding.

For example, small chairs as well as a few adult size chairs were provided for the carers to sit on so that they were at the children's eye level. The chairs were placed at the beginning of playgroup around the key play areas, so that carers were encouraged to form smaller groups near to where their children were playing. Carers here tended to follow their children from one activity to another and talk with the other carers who were supervising children at the same activity.

The play environment had also been designed with the help of child-care professionals to help make supervision easier for carers by cutting down on potential sources of conflict between children. For example, toys that could be fought over were kept to a minimum. Play activities included painting and pasting, sand and water play and climbing apparatus, all of which could involve children in parallel play.

Confrontation was therefore relatively infrequent, particularly since there was a high degree of supervision from carers, who tended to anticipate confrontation and use the potential source of dispute to teach their children to 'share'. However, on the days when large numbers of care-givers attended it was much more difficult for the carers to keep track of their children and confrontations were more frequent.

General demographic profile of participants

The vast majority of mothers who attended the suburban playgroups were living in a nuclear family with the father of their children. The majority of mothers had part-time, paid employment or were temporarily out of the workforce because they had just had a new baby. The pattern for mothers attending this playgroup was to spend one or two years at home with a new baby and then try to find part-time work that fitted in with family commitments, until another baby arrived. A few of the regulars had only stopped working for six weeks after their baby had been born, fitting part-time work in with the shift work of the father.

Amongst the regular attenders there was a single mother on a pension who had been associated with the centre as a volunteer from the time she left school. She was living in and out of a *de facto* relationship with the father of her two children and sometimes also with friends. Since having children, she had worked occasionally as a model and babysitter. There were other single mothers who attended less regularly. Two that I talked to during playgroup had lived for some time with their parents while waiting for the State Department of Housing to allocate them a house. There were also women who had been referred to the playgroup by health and welfare workers. However, no special provision was made for these women and they usually only attended once. They did not appear to find it easy to 'fit in' with this group.

The occupations of those attending this playgroup were extremely diverse. For example, there was a woman who took in ironing, another who worked as a barmaid; there was a Totalisator Agency Board (TAB) operator,[6] a psychology graduate, a number of office workers and teachers and nurses. The occupations that were cited by carers for their spouses were also extremely diverse. There were truck drivers, tradesmen, labourers, shift workers at the coal mine, a law clerk, a supervisor at the Broken Hill Proprietary (BHP) mining and industrial complex and an engineer. However, despite this diversity, the vast majority were nearly always in employment and owned or were buying their own home in the surrounding new housing estates.

All the carers who attended this venue were women, except for one father who was a regular attender. According to the women present, there had been other fathers on occasions in the past, and I was able to interview a father who had previously attended. Amongst the women carers there were always a few who were looking after other children as well as their own, either in an 'official' capacity as a family day care mother,[7] or informally in the sense that they were giving a friend a break, helping out another mother, or were involved in a reciprocal care arrangement.

There were also a number of women who accompanied mothers and carers to playgroup. For example, a grandmother who cared for her granddaughter three days a week, sometimes accompanied her daughter to playgroup as an outing for herself. A 20 year-old niece of one of the mothers accompanied her aunt so that she could help her aunt out with her two young children. There was also a woman who had shared a house for twelve months with the young child she brought to playgroup.

A neighbour of one of the regular mothers also attended. She had no children of her own, but enjoyed playgroup as a social outing for herself.

Volunteers also occasionally appeared to help out at playgroup. These came primarily from the local unemployed youth centre. The staff at the centre also informed me that students from the local high school sometimes did work experience here.

The suburban group's 'public face'

Apart from the playgroup committees, there was also an overall community management committee that administered the operation of the Family Support Service. This committee has been active since its formation eight years earlier. It consists of parents of the users of the playgroup, but it also has an advisory panel of professional health and welfare workers.

Over the years, the activities of this committee have included acting as a springboard for the establishment of a long day-care centre in one of the new housing estates. The committee is also often approached to provide representatives on local community planning committees. It has organized fun days to draw attention to various issues, such as the lack of playground and toilet facilities in the park in one of the local housing estates and must lobby each year for the continuation of the family support services that operate from the playgroup venue.

2 The 'kinship' playgroup

I chose the 'kinship' playgroup located at Bayswater because I had heard that this playgroup had a 'bad reputation'. I had found out about the group's reputation when I telephoned the local community neighbourhood centre to ask about researching a playgroup. The paid community worker, employed by the local council, informed me that a number of mothers had complained about the mothers in the kinship group failing to supervise their children adequately. She had decided to start up another playgroup in the community cottage for carers who wanted to be more involved in the activities of the children.

The community worker's report was confirmed when I met with the mothers who were setting up a playgroup in the community cottage. According to these mothers, the mothers meeting in the kinship group regarded playgroup simply as a chance to drink coffee and chat. They said that the kinship mothers did not appear to be concerned about what their children were doing. The mothers in the community cottage were setting up their own group which would focus more on the children's activities. I thought, then, that the group dynamics and interactive patterns of the kinship group might differ from the suburban group I had been observing and provide contrasts fruitful for concept building.

The kinship playgroup facilities are attached to the local Baby Health Centre and were built as a Commonwealth Employment Programme (CEP) project, initiated by a community-based committee comprising a number of health and welfare workers concerned with the lack of services for young families in the area. The initial project aimed to secure funding for a play leader/facilitator but the community health team leader decided it would be more beneficial for the mothers to learn to 'help themselves'. He was also reluctant to 'mix government departments'.[8]

General demographic profile of participants

Bayswater is more like a village than a town, in that the population density in the immediate area is quite low and stable. The local population, however, is comparably disadvantaged, comprising a high percentage of mobile home dwellers and a high proportion of people receiving government pensions.

The mothers at this venue had a noticeably lower socio-economic profile than the suburban playgroup. The majority had their first child between 16 and 19 years and were receiving the Supporting Parent's Benefit. Only two of the mothers who regularly attended were not on a government pension. Those on pensions either co-habited with the father of their child, who was often out of work, or they lived with their own mothers and moved in and out of a living arrangement with the father. I use the term 'kinship' to characterize this playgroup because of the heavy dependence of the majority of these women on their families of origin.

Only three of the mothers in this playgroup had paid work since having children. Two had occasionally been involved in caring for a friend's child while the friend worked and the other had worked for a few months as a shop assistant. The kinship mothers were far more likely than the suburban mothers to be 'full-time mothers'.

Most of these women had been involved in low-paid, low-status jobs before they had children and expressed little if any job satisfaction or personal fulfilment from this work. The occupations cited included check out operators, factory workers, shop assistants, a petrol-pump attendant and a receptionist. There was also a mother who had completed a secretarial course and had some nursing training.

The fathers of the children were in and out of the paid workforce. The occupations that the carers gave me for these men included labourers, a concreter, a fisherman and a dye setter. The husband of the mother who had some nursing experience was a local real estate agent and worked long hours. For the most part, however, the kinship fathers were unemployed. If not living with the mother of their children, they lived close by and came around to visit and take the children for outings.

Two of the regular attenders at this venue brought children other than their own while I was observing the playgroup, and there were also occasions when a mother kept an eye on another mother's child while she did some shopping in the supermarket across the street. A father also attended spasmodically. He lived with the mother of his two children in the housing commission home of his co-habitee's mother.

Although he told the mother he intended to come regularly to playgroup, he only appeared on two occasions, playing vigorously with his son and then disappearing as soon as his son tired of the game.

Organization of the group
This was a much smaller and a more close-knit group than the suburban group, reflecting the 'village-like' surroundings. The average group size was 8–10 carers and 10–12 children. Most of the regular attenders had known each other from school days and had become pregnant within a year or so of each other. I saw a few mothers arrive who were irregular attenders, but these, too, seemed to be known by the others in the group. There were a few mothers who had not known the regulars before attending the playgroup and had found out about the group from the community health nurse, but these were now on very friendly terms with the others in the group. Unlike the suburban playgroup, small groups did not form within the larger group so that carers either mixed in with the regulars or left the group to find another.

The kinship group was no longer run by a committee, although this had been the case when it was originally set up. There was a leader, Sue, who had been with the group for eight years. Sue kept the group going on a much more informal basis than the suburban group. She would simply talk to the carers each week about someone doing something special for the next week and if they were running short of funds, then they would hold a function to raise money. For example, they had recently held a fete at the playgroup venue to raise money for more playground equipment.

Sue told me that the mothers who attended this playgroup were the type to be put off by the level of organization that had occurred at first. Often, in the past, when a mother's turn to do a job had come up she would be too embarrassed to come that week. Sue had decided that a more 'laid back' atmosphere was more appropriate, along with the opportunity for mothers to talk to each other about their problems. She had attempted to provide them with this opportunity. 'When something needs doing, everyone pitches in', said Sue. 'Everyone here has had a really hard time and we all sit around and talk about it.'

This picture was confirmed during my visits. When carers arrived, they sat around the table inside and Sue made them a cup of coffee. They drank their coffee, had a smoke and chatted, mostly about problems they were having with their children or about their children's achievements. They also talked a lot about their problems with their personal relationships.

The first to arrive at playgroup would usually get a few toys out of the shed and scatter them around the yard. There were no chairs placed outside in the yard to encourage mothers and carers to sit outside, although there were big glass windows so that the children could be seen playing in the yard. Children were not actively supervised, but carers would intervene to comfort or chastise a child after they heard a child cry, or scream.

The equipment did not generally favour parallel play, so that cries and screams were relatively frequent, considering the much lower number of carers and children present. There were large and expensive pieces of equipment, such as a trampoline and a plastic slippery dip, that only one child at a time could play on and that led to many fights amongst the children. Play stations for parallel play, such as painting and playdough, were not set up as a matter of course each morning and there was very little equipment to encourage this sort of play or any play that would also involve the carers. For example, there was an expensive dolls' house but there were no dolls or play furniture for the children to play with the dolls' house. An expensive toy stove also stood in the corner, but there were no play utensils or playdough for the children to play with the stove.

Some form of craft activity usually took place once during the morning and this was the only time that the carers became involved in the children's activities. For example, paints were brought out as the special activity one morning. However, the paint was the expensive, commercial kind rather than the 'home-made' flour and colouring mixture that the suburban playgroup used. During the special activity, carers sat with their children and played with them. However, this activity usually only lasted a very short time and the carers were often left to play with the activity themselves and then spent a great deal of time cleaning it up.

When I first arrived, Sue drew my attention to a sign from the Playgroup Association that hung on the noticeboard. It read 'Every parent must help with activities and supervise their own children. Remember that YOU are responsible for the safety and discipline of your own child at playgroup.' She said that she showed it to all new parents when they first arrived. However, unlike the parents who attended the suburban playgroup, where the same rule applied, parents here interpreted this rule as intervening only when absolutely necessary.

The kinship group's 'public face'

Although there had been attempts to set up a management committee in the past, these had been largely unsuccessful. However, while I was visiting the group they became involved in a public discussion on talk-back radio. When I arrived one morning, the group was huddled around the coffee table, discussing a circular that one of the mothers had received from a friend. The circular was drawing attention to the 'fact' that the New South Wales government was about to introduce a law making it illegal for anyone to mind children if not licensed by DOCS. The mothers were in a very agitated state and one of them suggested they call up the local radio station. This resulted in a mother discussing the issue over talk-back radio. The radio announcer took an interest in the issue and called up the Minister concerned, who reassured the mothers that the new law would not affect their private child-minding arrangements.

3 The 'alternative' playgroup

I got to know about an 'alternative' playgroup through a friend who had organized the group through a local birthing association. Their group met in a park, located near the Central Business District of Newcastle, New South Wales. The location, however, is a less significant factor in the group's formation than the fact that the participants shared common 'counter-cultural' ideals. I felt that observations of this group might prove fruitful for drawing out the effects of alternative ideas on the group's dynamics and interactive patterns.

In this group there were only four or five regular attenders. Two of these were accompanied by their partner, who in both cases was the father of their children. A number of others appeared on different occasions and at different times throughout the morning. This group was also very close-knit and even those who attended spasmodically were given a rousing welcome. As well as their own children, the mothers in this group sometimes brought at least one extra child; a niece or nephew or the child of a friend. One of the regulars often brought her niece. She cared for her niece on a regular basis on this day while the mother worked in the school canteen.

General demographic profile of participants

It is difficult to characterize this group according to similar occupational criteria or income levels. Members of this group had very diverse life experience and occupations. However, group members did tend to have a higher level of formal education than either the suburban or kinship groups and even if currently unemployed, they did not appear to be overly concerned by their status as dependants.

Two couples who attended regularly were currently living on unemployment benefits. Although unemployed, these couples did not appear to suffer any lessening of their self-esteem by having to depend on welfare benefits. They regarded being on a pension during the early child-rearing years favourably. It provided them with the opportunity to spend more time with their children, which they felt was more important than paid work. One of these mothers had travelled extensively overseas and worked in a variety of occupations including barmaid, cleaning and child-care work in a creche in Holland, where she had met her partner, who was a photographer. The other had left school at 15 and lived on a farm with her sister. Before having children she had worked as a cleaner and as a barmaid. Her partner, although now on an invalid pension, was a journalist before an accident left him unable to continue this work. He had gone back to university and gained honours in English literature and worked occasionally as a tutor in Indian culture.

Two other regular attenders were trained teachers, although they were currently 'full-time mothers' being financially supported by their husbands who were also teachers. One had also worked in numerous other occupations. She had been a bank clerk, a secretary, an artist's model and had run a youth hostel together with her husband. Although now teaching, her husband had also worked as a builder and as a handyman. The other regular attender lived on her own with her three young children. She got occasional work at a local radio station.

It was the group's shared ideals that were most significant in bringing the members of this group together. The most important shared ideals related to what they considered were natural methods of birth and child-rearing. In particular, there was a strong belief in the importance of mothering in laying the foundations for a secure and responsible adult. Other issues which linked this playgroup related to their concern for the environment, their general disregard for mass consumption and high achievement in a materialistic sense. There was also strong support expressed for the Steiner school, a private school that emphasizes fostering the creativity and individual abilities of children in a farm-like atmosphere. Unusual children's names also characterized this group. Names were selected with a great deal of care in order to accentuate the couple's individuality and the individuality of each child.

A number of the members of this group had experienced alternative living arrangements before having children. One of the fathers had lived in a community in India and another had lived in a community in Holland. Most of the mothers had shared houses with friends in the past. One mother had lived with her sister's family after leaving home at 15. In addition, two couples had lived for nearly 12 months with the mother's family of origin after having children and one mother lived on her own with her three children. However, even though reservations were expressed in conversation about nuclear family living arrangements, this was currently the predominant arrangement for those attending the group while I was an observer.

Organization of playgroup
Josie is a member of a local birthing association, and started this playgroup for 'purely social' reasons. She put an ad in the association's newsletter, welcoming any interested parents into the group which met one morning each week in a park. When I first met with the group, they were having their first winter meeting, having previously met each week at the beach. Josie told me that it is much easier having playgroup at an outdoor venue because there is less for the children to fight over and plenty for the children to do with the minimum of parental intervention.

The first venue was located next to a playground, but the playground equipment caused a number of fights between the children so at Josie's suggestion they moved the group the next week to another park which was further away from any playground equipment. When the mothers arrived, they spread out a big rug and sat down together. The children sat on their mothers' laps, or close by their carer. Gradually, the children moved away to play on the grass, returning to sit on their mothers' laps, or to be near their carer at various intervals.

The mothers on the rug paid a lot of attention to the children of other mothers, particularly the babies. Occasionally one of the mothers would get up to follow her child, or play with the children with a ball or chase them up and down the hill. When the children eventually wandered off to the playground, one or two of the mothers would volunteer to follow and supervise while the others remained with the babies on the rug.

Over at the playground, the mothers would assist each child on the play equipment. They would push them on swings, catch them on the slippery dip and help push the see-saw up and down. When the children wandered away, there was little attempt made to restrain them. Instead, a mother or two would follow the children around the park and eventually lead them back to the others on the rug.

The alternative group's 'public face'

This group was part of a larger birthing association, although not all of those who dropped in and out were members of this association. They all, however, had a lively interest in the public debates over home birth and natural methods of healing and there was often discussion about these issues. Group members sometimes wrote letters to the editor of the newspaper and they were all involved in monitoring the media and producing the association's newsletter.

Method outline

When I began attending each playgroup, I informed those I spoke to of the general nature of my research. I did not have a child at playgroup, but this proved to be an advantage, since being responsible for a particular child would have been a distraction. However, I did find that my earlier experience as a member of a number of playgroups was invaluable. I drew on this past experience to find some common ground with carers in all three groups.

When I arrived at playgroup, I moved around the group and recorded who was present and which children they were responsible for minding. This gave me the opportunity to meet each attender personally and elicit demographic information and information about their living arrangements. Many mothers volunteered information at this stage about their subjective experience as a mother and primary carer.

Becoming engaged in conversation was the best way to observe the interaction in the group without appearing to be a detached outsider. I also participated in the activities of the group to the extent that I assisted in setting up activities, cutting up fruit for the children and helping the mothers to clean up. Joining in with the play activities of the children was another way of blending in with the group.

After I got to know a few of the regular attenders, I also began to take the initiative with their children. For example, I helped them with tasks such as washing their hands and tying their shoelaces and I read them stories and became involved in their play. I also offered to supervise a toddler if the mother was busy with a baby, or hold a baby if the mother was engaged elsewhere.

Often while I was engaged in conversation I would observe an incident that drew my attention. On these occasions I did not wish to draw attention to myself as an observer by writing the incident down as it was happening, but I did manage to record some of the specifics of the incident in the book that I carried around to record who was present. As soon as playgroup ended, I used these notes to elaborate more detailed field notes. Altogether, I observed and recorded 36 hours of 'face-to-face' playgroup interaction.

My observations focused on the following questions:

1 Group Interaction
 (a) What are the norms of each group?
 (b) How are these norms enforced?
 (c) How is conflict handled within the group?
2 Interaction within the dyad
 (a) How is the agency of the child evident in the dyad's interaction?
 (b) How is conflict handled within the dyad?

After each period of observation I wrote up fieldnotes which included my own reflections on the events I had witnessed, as well as a detailed description of the events themselves. As my research progressed, I began to anticipate what were becoming regular patterns of interaction. These became all the more obvious when they failed to eventuate. The contrasts provided by these incidents drew my attention and refocused my observations and reflections.

The semi-structured interviews
As the research progressed I thought that more formal, semi-structured interviews with a sample from each group would allow me to elaborate on the interactive patterns that I was observing and give parents the opportunity to describe their subjective experience of these situations. As I drew up the interview schedule, I thought that it would also be valuable to interview a sample of fathers in order to address the question of gender difference in parent–child interaction. However, this proved to be very time consuming, since I had to interview the fathers individually, in their own homes. I was able to interview the mothers in the suburban and kinship groups in a vacant room at the playgroup venues and I already felt at ease with these respondents. The number of fathers is therefore very limited and includes no kinship fathers because these men were difficult to track down and very reluctant to be interviewed.

There were 35 respondents altogether. There were 21 from the suburban group, eight from the kinship group and six from the alternative group. This included nine men, six from the suburban group and three from the alternative group.

The key issues which I discussed with parents were:

1 Their parenting expectations and ideals.
2 How these were influenced by the reality of child-rearing.
3 How parents learnt to care for their children.
4 Whether they sought advice; who was most helpful.
5 Parent–child confrontation.
6 The effect of different social environments on parent–child interaction.
7 Their expectations of how other parents should behave in social situations.
8 Ideal alternative care.
9 Parents' experience of 'diffuse care' living arrangements.

In the following three chapters, I have organized the ethnographic material around three general questions, each of which is the focus for a chapter:

1 How do maternal attitudes differ? How are they affected by the group's dynamics?
2 How does the mother come to understand the needs of her own particular child?
3 What is the outcome of maternal-infant conflict and how is the outcome affected by the predominant maternal attitude?

5 // Maternal attitudes

The mother as primary carer

The aim of this chapter is to describe the different maternal attitudes that existed in each group and the normative context which sustained them. What is of immediate interest are the similarities in the normative context of all three groups. These similarities relate to the fact that in every case it was the mother who was the child's primary carer, at least in the child's earliest weeks.

In every instance in the study it was the mother who initially took the personal responsibility for her child's care, even if the father was prepared to share the care, or became the primary carer at a later date. There were two cases of 'role swapping' present in the sample in which the father had been the primary carer for about 12 months. Neither had been responsible for the care of their newborn, but had taken over the responsibility of primary care from the mother. In one case, the child was 12 months old when the father became the primary carer and in the other case, the child was 6 months old and the father's second child. When asked how they had come to know what the needs of their child were when they first took over as primary carers, both fathers replied that they had learned this, or 'picked up bits and pieces', from the mother. The infants were already in a routine by the time these fathers had to care for them. This meant that they were able to continue on with the routines that the mother had established with the child.

This also occurred in another case where the mother and father organized their work commitments to enable at least one of them to be home to care for their child. The father readily conceded that he relied on his wife to tell him what the infant required. He started out caring for his infant on his own for very short periods, taking instructions from the mother and slowly building up his confidence to the stage where he could care for his infant for longer periods of time. Like the 'role swap' parents, it was the mother who actually did the work of interpreting and organizing the infant's early patterns of care into a relatively predictable pattern that gave both her and her husband the confidence necessary to share the infant's care.

Other fathers in the sample had a similar experience with caring for their infants on their own. They tended to only mind their infant for short periods and received instructions on what the baby would need during this time from the mother. Mothers left their infants for short periods when they felt reasonably confident that their infant would not require their own monitoring for that period. This generally meant that the mothers had managed to introduce some element of predictability into their day, even if this was subsequently altered.

There were also two cases in the alternative group in which the father was at home with the mother for the early period of care-giving. These couples expressed the ideal of 'shared parenting' in that both the mother and the father wanted to spend time caring for their children. However, in both cases the mothers held a very strong moral commitment to the ideal that all their infants' 'needs' should be immediately gratified. Since the only response to the infant's crying was to put the baby to the breast, it proved impossible for the fathers to share care equally. Even as the infants grew older, the pattern of gratifying the infant with the breast was so firmly established, that when both the father and mother were present, the infants demanded their mother when they became distressed. The fathers felt very inadequate about being able to satisfy their child's demands.

As Allan, one of the alternative fathers who expressed the ideal of shared care, put it:

> because Josie's always breast-fed I've never been able to give the babies a bottle, and that would probably make me feel more adequate, but I mean, because they've been breast-fed they won't accept anything else . . . having the breast is so wonderful, you know.

The two fathers who spent time alone with their child as primary carers did begin to take on their own understanding of their child's needs when left to care for the child themselves. During their time as primary carers, they were the ones to consider the needs of the child from the child's point of view. Ross, for example, spoke of his wife, who was working full time, as having 'no comprehension' of the dangers that young children were likely to get into. He was the one who put himself in the place of the child and tried to anticipate potential accidents.

The important point to understand here is that mothers apparently 'know' what it is their infant 'needs' because they are the ones who are usually responsible for the early period of primary care. Because they are held personally responsible for their infant's care, they also perceive themselves as being the ones who should 'know' what it is that their infant 'needs'. It is this feeling of personal responsibility that leads the mother to perform this early, interpretive work with the infant. There is no reason why the father, or any other adult could not interpret the needs of the infant if they were to accept the primary responsibility for the infant's care.

However, as other research in the area of early primary care demonstrates, it is extremely difficult to locate fathers who have had the primary responsibility for the care of their child from birth. Moreover, this is an area which is extremely resistant to change through government intervention strategies. Consider the fact that even in Sweden, where the State has attempted 'to sell role sharing as an ideal for men' (Haas 1982) and provided structural support for fathers to take time off work to be with their newborn infants, no sample of 'shared parenting' triads have, as yet, included fathers who had been primary carers to their newborn infants (Lamb et al. 1982; Hwang 1986).

If the mother inevitably proved to be the one responsible for early primary care in the nuclear families in the sample, how did they fare in situations where group care was possible?

Communal and diffuse caregiving

There were a number of living arrangements that were conducive to 'communal care' in the sample. In these situations there were a number of adult carers involved in the early primary care of a particular child, and more than one attachment figure. However, even here, care was usually taken to give a particular person the primary responsibility for defining the child's needs at any one point in time. In this sample, this person was always the infant's mother. Attempts by other adults to act as the child's 'interpreter', as often happened with the kinship mothers who lived with their own mothers, became an intense source of tension.

Roslyn was a regular attender of the suburban group. She was not the child's mother but had lived with the child's parents for the first 12 months of the child's life. Her living arrangements were conducive to 'communal care' in that all the adults involved participated in the care of the child and the child was attached to each adult. Roslyn had moved out to live on her own when the child was 12 months old, but still retained contact with the family and took the child on outings by herself.

The child was 3 years of age when I observed them at playgroup and she demonstrated a great attachment to Roslyn. However, according to Roslyn, it was the mother who had always made the decisions on what the child needed. Like the 'role swap' fathers, Roslyn told me how she had 'always allowed them to tell me, to guide me on what to do with her . . . Kathy [the mother] mostly'. She was also aware of the possibility of her intervention causing tension with the child's parents and told me how she 'took a back seat' as far as chastising the child was concerned when her parents were around. However, she was quite prepared to discipline the child when the parents were not present and she was the responsible person.

In the kinship group there were a number of young, single mothers living with their own mothers. Although the young mothers welcomed the instrumental assistance and emotional support of their own mothers, and actively sought this support and advice, they deeply resented their mothers' inclination to define the child's needs for them. This was a source of great tension.

In Sue's case, for example:

Michael and I broke up on the Saturday night. Anyway, I moved back in with mum. Well, from the Sunday morning on it was just 'Sue, don't you think you should change Tammy?' 'Sue, what's Max doing?' 'Sue, don't you think Tammy needs . . .' 'Sue, don't you think you're breast-feeding Max too often . . . ?' and you know 'Now in my day that never happened, and in my day we did it this way.' So I lasted there for two days and I moved out to the garage and set up a stove and that in the garage and just went inside for baths and water and that. I just couldn't handle it. She's been great. I can't knock her you know. She's always willing to babysit and everything for me but . . . it was like going back to when I was a little girl, you know.

Many of the young mothers in this situation offered similar accounts of living with their mothers. They appreciated the instrumental help and affection that their own parents were able to provide, and often sought their advice but they did not appreciate having their own mothers' interpretation of the child's needs imposed upon them. The tension that this situation aroused in these young mothers led them to actively seek a situation where they could be more independent, living apart from their mothers yet still close enough to obtain the benefit of their mother's considerable support.

However, there were individual cases where extended family living did not appear to engender tension. There were isolated cases in both the kinship and suburban group where grandparents were portrayed as very understanding and restrained. Being aware of the potential tension, these grandparents managed to overcome any desire to intervene in their children's child-rearing practices. One mother in the suburban group, for example, lived with her parents for a while when her house was being built. Like Roslyn in the example of the communal household, her parents had been conscious about the possibility of undermining the daughter's desire to bring her children up in her own way. According to this informant, they only offered advice if asked.

It seems, therefore, that recognizing the particularities of a child, in a continuous and consistent manner, sets certain limitations upon the ideals expressed in the notion of 'shared' primary care. Parents who have set out to 'share care' must be very familiar with this problem. The literature certainly is. For example, Bennett Berger's (1981) study of child-rearing on 'New Age' communes in California describes how the care of infants while requiring 'constant monitoring' is left up to their mothers, even though members are influenced by feminist rhetoric regarding traditional sex-role stereotypes. Any communal aspects of care at this stage are in the hands of the group of 'mothers-with-children'.

The difficulty in 'sharing' early nurturing activity 'equally' arises from the ideals of autonomy and individuality that our Western culture holds so dearly. Only one person at a time can build up an idiosyncratic pattern of communication with a pre-verbal child and give consistency and continuity to the patterns that evolve. Psychologists have depicted early nurturing as occurring in the context of 'a singular care-giving relationship'. While their description of this relationship is useful for the Western context, it should not be regarded as a universal.

The singular caregiving relationship

Psychologists frequently use the phrase 'a singular care-giving relationship' to describe the sequence of behaviours initiated by the infant to elicit from the mother the feeling that she has a unique relationship with her child (Lewis and Lee-Painter 1974). Most writers in this area of infant development recognize today that the person involved in this unique, primary relationship need not be the biological mother (Rutter 1981). They use the term 'primary carer' or 'primary care-giver' to denote the fact that this person may be any adult, male or female, who takes on the personal responsibility for a particular infant's care.

The psychological literature depicts the singular care-giving relationship as fundamental to the development of the unique patterns of communication of the maternal-infant dyad. These patterns of communication are understood within the context of a learning model, where the infant's behaviour sustains the proximity of the primary carer and selectively reinforces appropriate care-giving behaviour (Bell 1974). The singular care-giving relationship is unique in that a pattern of communication is set up between the primary carer and child which is idiosyncratic to each pair (Schaffer and Dunn 1979; Rutter 1981).

This pattern of communication depends upon intense, affective exchanges which develop over time and are highly personalized. The conclusion drawn from these studies is that the primary carer must be prepared to enter into an enduring bond with a particular child, and be personally committed to providing this child with a continuity of care.

Psychological research has described qualitative differences existing between the child's relationship with the primary carer and the child's other adult relationships. However, it is sometimes implied in the sociological literature that the concept of the singular care-giving relationship means, in effect, that maternal care-giving should be 'exclusive'.[1] The singular care-giving relationship is not 'exclusive' in the sense that this is the only relationship the child may enter into. Pre-verbal infants may well have a variety of relationships with other adults, with whom affective bonds develop (Pedersen 1980; Lamb et al. 1982).

The distinction that I make between the singular care-giving relationship and the other relationships that the child enters into in the early years is based on the orientation of the primary carer towards understanding the needs of a particular child. In a singular care-giving relationship, a particular adult takes on the personal responsibility for meeting the needs of a particular infant and as a prerequisite for meeting these needs, must first of all define them. The other relationships that the child enters into may well provide the child with affection and social stimulation and be of great assistance to the primary carer, but it is in the context of the singular care-giving relationship that the infant's actions are defined as 'needs'. In my view, this is an important reason why mothers tend to prefer alternative care arrangements which can ensure some continuity and consistency of care.[2]

The fundamental social condition for a singular care-giving relationship to exist is the acceptance by an adult of the personal responsibility for the care and well-being of a particular child. Care-giving then becomes an intersubjective process in which action sequences are mutually effective. This is a very important point to grasp. Action within the early care-giving relationship is mutually effective, that is, the actions of the child produce effects in the carer which are just as relevant for investigation as the carer's actions on the child.

It is this element of mutual effectiveness that distinguishes care-giving within a singular care-giving relationship from care-giving that is task orientated, as in nursing or teaching. In nursing, for example, the infant's needs are defined and met by staff strategically. Nurses need to be interchangeable. However, in a singular care-giving relationship, the carer and infant develop an idiosyncratic pattern of communication that is grounded in highly affective interchanges that develop over time. The mutual effectiveness of this action context allows the child to contribute to the definition of his or her own 'needs'. Primary carers in this situation are not easily interchangeable.

Pam, a trained and experienced midwife, expresses this distinction as the outcome of feeling personally responsible for an individual child:

> I suppose it's when they're crying and you don't know why they're crying and you're trying to figure it out . . . I mean you are responsible for caring for it, I mean, there's no-one else you could say, here you are, this baby's crying, what are you going to do, you know. Unless you've got family and I didn't have family close by . . . When I was at work and there was a baby that cried you were sort of more objective, you know. You didn't worry as much

I suppose; you did all the things you thought, you know, to calm it, and then after that you thought well, you know, just leave it . . .

However, as I have pointed out, nurturing within a singular care-giving relationship need not be regarded as a universal. It simply reflects the Western values of autonomy and individuality. We can see how 'group' care might differ by studying the nurturing patterns in a culture such as the Kibbutz. Bettelheim (1969) and Tiger and Shepher (1975) studied child-rearing here, and their studies provide an interesting contrast to nurturing within a singular care-giving relationship. Unlike 'New Age' communes which have emerged primarily for the purpose of 'self-actualization'[3] the Kibbutz movement's primary objective is the survival of the community itself. Facilitating the development of the child's individuality is not a deliberate goal of child-rearing. This has important implications for the patterns of infant care that have developed in the Kibbutz.

According to Bettelheim and Tiger and Shepher, most mothers do breast-feed in the Kibbutz but it is an instrumental act of giving food and affection. Nurses, or metapelet, are responsible for the infants' primary care. The infants' needs are organized from the start into a routine which is applied uniformly to all infants in the nursery. The mother comes in from work every four hours to feed and nurture her child as part of this routine.

In this situation, mothers do not experience themselves as responsible for the primary care of their child. But neither are the particularities of Kibbutz children recognized in their child-rearing patterns. Here, the infants' 'needs' *are* objectively defined, scientifically, and met uniformly. The attributes we associate with individuality, such as self-assertiveness, are not highly valued. Interestingly enough though, even here, where the ideology of the community is directly opposed to the idea that a mother should take personal responsibility for her own infant's care, a mother may begin to develop a singular care-giving relationship with her child if left to care for her child herself in the early weeks. Bettelheim (1969: 127) informs us, for example, that if there is a sickness in the nursery and the mother must care for her infant herself for a few weeks, she will generally find it more difficult to return the child to the nursery.

The point that needs to be stressed here, is that once an individual carer is left to care for a particular child and experiences herself as personally responsible for that child's care, the ability of the child to effect the primary carer and induce highly affective responses from the primary carer becomes a crucial factor in explaining subsequent care-giving patterns. The child's agency, or the ability of the child to shape the care-giving behaviour of the care-giver, must be taken into account. At this point, what needs to be explained is why anyone, and the mother in particular, would place themselves in a singular care-giving relationship with a particular child.

The normative context of maternal attitudes

The mother's responsibility for gratification

The essential condition for a singular care-giving relationship to develop is an individual adult's acceptance of the personal responsibility for the welfare of a particular child. What the psychological literature is unable to explain is why it is overwhelmingly the mother who accepts the personal responsibility for the care of her child and enters into this relationship. The answer to this question lies in two broad normative expectations of mothering that were generally held by mothers across all three groups. The first of these relates to the mother's responsibility for gratification.

Many mothers in the study were conscious of a social expectation that as the infant's mother, she should know the needs of her own infant and be able to satisfy these. A majority had held this belief themselves before giving birth to their first child. They expressed surprise at what was involved in caring for a baby, since they entered into motherhood with the belief that the needs of their infant would be self-evident.

What they discovered when they began to care for their infants was that they first had to find out what their infants did need. Mothers went through an initial period of intense preoccupation with the actions of their infant, attempting to discover what it was their infant was trying to tell them they wanted. Mothers did see this early period of nurturing as a trial-and-error learning process, whereby they should be able to arrive at the correct answer if only they could learn to 'read' the cues of their infant correctly.

In searching for the correct answer, mothers sought advice, particularly from their own mothers, but also from other relatives and friends and the Early Childhood Nurses working in Baby Health Centres. They were also given plenty of unsolicited advice! There were some interesting variations between the groups here.

The kinship mothers relied very heavily on advice from their own mothers, which often came in the guise of actual, physical assistance, as the following exchange between myself and a kinship mother, Karen illustrates:

Chris: Did you have any idea what it was going to be like having a baby?
Karen: No.
Chris: What happened, then, when you got home from the hospital?
Karen: I didn't know it was going to be so much work. Tired all the time, you gotta spend all your time with them, do everything for them, everything they need.
Chris: Did you have any idea how to look after him?
Karen: No. Lucky mum was there.

Chris: So your mum was a big help?

Karen: Yeah, she was great. She'd get up and do some night feeds while I had a sleep, things like that. Do some washing for me, and iron some of the clothes. We'd take turns at things. She'd mind him while I went out sometimes and things like that.

Chris: Did she sort of tell you what to do?

Linda: No, No, No. Only If I asked her. If I didn't know how to do it I'd ask her.

Mothers in the suburban group also depended heavily on their own mothers, who were greatly missed if not available. Margaret, a suburban mother who had been a ward of the state and fostered out as a child, believed that a lot of the problems she experienced nurturing her own children were the outcome of not having a mother of her own:

Chris: Could anything have prepared you, do you think, for looking after your child?

Margaret: Oh, I did reading, but not having a mother was the biggest thing, I think. Not having someone there that you could, you know, ask little things about . . .

However, mothers could also be regarded as 'interfering', particularly if they gave advice without being asked and without providing the advice in the context of giving actual, physical assistance and emotional support. What is interesting here is that the more educated mothers, particularly those well read in psychology and alternative spiritualities, found their ideals now clashed with their mothers' way of doing things. They were also far more likely to reject the Early Childhood Nurses' advice. But this does not mean they did not need 'advice'. On the contrary, it seemed to me that they were far more reliant on books and often retained contact with their alternative midwives for advice on child-rearing. They also sought out friends with common ideals and value systems with whom they could discuss their nurturing concerns.

Even though mothers are well-known to engage in this intensive seeking of advice, the belief that mothers will instinctively know what their infant needs remains a popular image of motherhood, reinforced in the child-rearing literature that the suburban mothers overwhelmingly referred to once their baby was born. For example, in the 1983 edition of *Our Babies*, published by the New South Wales Health Department and given out to all new mothers, they are told that the old way of rearing babies according to schedules goes against the 'intuitive wish' of the mother to respond to the baby's cries appropriately. The 'new way' advocated arises from a 'better understanding of child development'. The new way begins with the idea:

that if parents trust what nature has given them, both in their babies and in themselves, the whole business will be not only more successful but more relaxed and enjoyable (although needing patience and many skills). (Department of Health 1983: 18)

Another popular work mentioned by numerous suburban mothers was Christopher Green's book, *Toddler Taming* (1984). Like many popular versions of the 'good-enough mother' described by object-relations psychoanalytic writers, Christopher Green believes that the infant's needs are self-evident and should be immediately gratified by the mother. In the opening pages, he writes:

The aim in the first year is to develop a secure and trusting child, who has a secure and trusting relationship with his parents. When he is hungry he should be fed; when he is frightened he should be comforted; and when he cries he should be cuddled. You cannot spoil a baby in the first year of life. (p. 2)

The popular ideal of the good mother as someone who knows what her infant needs and gratifies these immediately arose in the first instance as a reaction to child-rearing trends advocating the regimentation of child-care according to scientifically formulated principles. These scheduling techniques were made popular about 60 years ago in the work of Truby King, whose main concern was to eradicate infant mortality by managing the nurturing activity of mothers (Dally 1982; Reiger 1985).

There were also other important cultural influences in the 1960s which reinforced the change in child-rearing ideals from scientific management to the reliance on maternal instinct. For example, Bernice Martin (1981: 25) describes the 1960s as being characterized by 'anti-structural symbolism' which involved a counter-cultural attack on all forms of boundaries, limits, roles and conventions. Martin associates this movement with the Left and argues that the Left adopted the idealization of the self-defining individual and expressive values in a counter-cultural movement which was in contrast to the instrumentalization and bureaucratization of this particular stage of capitalist development (p. 18).

These child-centred ideals are now very much mainstream, although held with much greater moral fervour by the alternative couples. They reinforce the mother's perception of herself as being the one who should know what her child 'needs'. If breast-feeding 'on demand' the mother is also likely to experience herself as being the only one who can satisfy the infant's 'needs', since in the early months, putting the baby to the breast is the most common way of comforting, as well as nourishing, the infant. Thus, the infant also comes to perceive the mother as its source of gratification (or frustration). As we shall see in the next chapter, these child-rearing ideals come into conflict with the mother's own interests and she is frequently required to make adjustments to these ideals and re-define their meaning.

The mother's feeling of responsibility for her child's 'need' gratification is also reinforced by the social practice of handing crying babies back to their mothers for comfort. During my observations I noticed that other women occasionally cuddled another baby and sometimes attempted to console a crying child. However, if the child's cries continued the mother was always sought. Other adults tend to get very agitated in the company of a crying infant. Thus, mothers often feel under a lot of pressure to bring the crying under control. This is particularly the case with new mothers, some of whom experience this pressure with a great deal of anxiety.

Mothers tended to feel very inadequate when they did not 'know' what was wrong with their child and could not comfort their child. Julie, for example, was a mother who found the expectation that she should know what was wrong with her child intolerable. She expressed great anxiety at being unable to 'control' her child and felt that people expected her to be able to do this. She told me how she felt when her 6 week-old baby began to cry at a Tupperware party and she was unable to console him:

> I was more upset about the fact that he was crying and I was a new mother and I couldn't control him, and people were coming up to me and saying, 'what's the matter with the baby', you know, 'do you want me to take him', and I just felt totally inadequate and useless. I just felt like I was totally fooled.

Thus, the generally accepted assumption that babies are born with certain physical and emotional needs that mothers will immediately recognize and be able to gratify, intensifies the mothers early preoccupation with trying to understand her own particular child. She cannot hope to meet the needs of her child until she finds out, exactly, what it is her child does need.

The mother's responsibility for social behaviour

As well as feeling personally responsible for satisfying their child's needs, the mothers in the study also felt personally responsible for the social behaviour of their child. Playgroup norms sustained this belief. For example, in all three playgroups, it was generally accepted that no mother should chastise another mother's child if the mother was present and they all expected the mother to intervene if their child was involved in anti-social behaviour. Mothers whose children were overly distressed, or engaged in anti-social behaviour tended to experience a great deal of embarrassment, or shame because they held themselves to be responsible. The child's failing was experienced as their own. Their embarrassment then reinforced their perception of themselves as personally responsible and prompted them to intervene in the situation.

For example, one morning I was sitting with Jill at the playdough table. Her son, Damion, was really trying his mother's patience. Every tool that the little girl next to him picked up, Damion wanted. Jill tried to be reasonable, offering him other ones that were exactly the same and pointing out that he could have Sarah's one when Sarah was finished with it. Damion threw all the alternatives away, crying loudly and demanding the one that Sarah had. Jill was getting more and more agitated and told me how terribly embarrassing her son's behaviour was for her. She was on the verge of packing up and going home when Sarah finished playing with the playdough and went off somewhere else to play.

However, although the mothers from all three playgroups expected a mother to intervene when their child was involved in anti-social acts, not all mothers felt embarrassed, or distressed when their child had to be disciplined in a public place. The kinship mothers were noticeably less embarrassed by their children's behaviour at playgroup and their interviews confirmed this observation. They felt more relaxed in social situations because their socializing tended to be with people with whom they could just 'be themselves'.

There were also differences in the way in which mothers from each group talked about their feelings for mothers whose children were engaging in anti-social behaviour. A number of suburban mothers mentioned feeling sympathetic to mothers involved in these situations. A few also mentioned how much more tolerant they were now of children's anti-social acts and understood how difficult it sometimes was to control a child. In contrast, two of the kinship mothers told me how angry they got with mothers who 'did nothing' to discipline their child, but allowed their child 'to get away with it'.

Expecting the mother to deal with anti-social behaviour also seemed to be the norm in the alternative group, although this group tried to avoid having to confront the whole issue of anti-social behaviour by planning their meetings in an environment where anti-social acts between children would be least likely to occur. However, on the first morning that I visited this group, a 2 year-old boy kicked a younger child in the head. Most of the mothers saw the incident, but said nothing to the boy or to the mother, who had her back to her son at the time. It appeared that these mothers were trying to avoid embarrassing the mother. A short time later, one of the mothers referred to the boy's behaviour as 'street wise'; a phrase which portrayed his actions in a more favourable light.

These norms were held by all mothers across all three groups. Their existence helps to explain why it is the mother who enters into the singular care-giving relationship with the child. Once in a singular care-giving relationship, the child also becomes a powerful agent affecting the mother's perception of herself as the one who 'knows' what it is her child 'needs'. However, even though all the children in my study were reared within a singular care-giving relationship, different maternal attitudes could still be detected in each group.

Maternal attitudes

In all three groups it was possible to detect the preoccupation of mothers towards trying to understand the needs of their own particular child in the very early stages of mothering. I call this preoccupation the maternal attitude towards understanding, or 'taking the attitude of the child'. There was usually an intensive period of caring around the clock for a newborn infant. During this early period, the mother became preoccupied with trying to understand what the infant's actions meant. As a result of the mother's often intensive efforts to understand her infant, each mother was able to describe the development of an idiosyncratic pattern of care, to which she could refer more or less confidently to explain the actions of her child.

However, as the infant grew older, there were marked differences in maternal attitudes between the three groups. In the suburban group, mothers tended to retain the orientation towards understanding, so that they were often able to anticipate and avoid potentially distressing situations for their child. This orientation towards mothering gave mothers the scope to evaluate the child's actions, differentiating 'needs' from 'demands' and giving themselves room to negotiate space for competing sets of interests.

In the kinship group, however, the predominant maternal attitude towards understanding became more coercive once mother and infant were settled into a fairly predictable daily routine. Although these mothers also developed idiosyncratic patterns of care with their newborn, once their baby had settled down, mothers adopted more of a strategic attitude towards caring for their child. In the main, these mothers did not make the intensive efforts to understand their child, so that their child would avoid becoming distressed. Neither did they attempt to understand their child so that confrontation between themselves and their child would be kept to a minimum. Instead, they tended to console their child *after* distressing situations, and relied on more coercive means of directing their child's behaviour.

The alternative mothers differed again, in that the orientation towards understanding that continued on in the suburban group throughout the early child-rearing years, tended to be disrupted until approximately the child's third year. This occurred because of the very firm child-centred ideals held by the alternative mothers. Early attempts to understand their infant lapsed into a pattern in which mothers gave their infants the breast in response to all their infant's signals. The crystallization of this stimulus-response pattern of interaction meant that it was only the mother who could gratify the child. Eventually infants began to take the initiative in this stimulus–response mode of interaction, gratifying themselves by taking the breast whenever they desired.

The particular orientation I call 'taking the attitude of the child' arises in conditions where the mother and child come to clearly distinguish two separate perspectives and two separate sets of interests. This line tended to be blurred for the alternative dyads. It only became clearly distinguishable when a direct confrontation occurred between the mother and child. In the alternative group, direct confrontation with their child tended to occur later, with far greater emotional intensity. The event which usually brought it about was weaning, when the child was in his or her third year. However, confrontation was sometimes also forced upon the alternative mothers as a result of the child's anti-social acts towards other children.

Thus, even though all the dyads in the study were in a singular care-giving relationship, there were still great differences in the maternal attitudes of members of each group. Maternal attitudes were largely shaped by the very different child-rearing ideals held by members in each playgroup.

Child-rearing ideals in the suburban group

The majority of suburban mothers had undertaken ante-natal classes and had generally decided before the birth how they were going to feed their new baby. They were very much influenced by the popular child-rearing literature in this regard, which stressed the benefits of breast-feeding and advocated an approach called feeding the baby 'on demand'. Only two suburban mothers I spoke to had decided to bottle-feed from birth, and only two of my respondents had made the conscious decision before having the baby to fit the baby into a pre-formulated 'schedule', or daily routine of feeding.

Child-centred literature has, then, become mainstream to the extent that the majority of these suburban mothers accepted the wisdom of breast-feeding and an approach to care-giving that directed the mother's attention to working out the child's needs from the child's point of view, rather than simply attempting to impose a routine on the child as had been advocated in manuals of advice to mothers earlier this century.[4]

However, child-centred ideals were not as strongly adhered to by these mothers, compared to the alternative group. The suburban mothers tended to be more pragmatic in their outlook towards child-rearing and were able to adjust their beliefs about what they thought was good for their child to their own particular circumstances at any point in time. An important effect of having more vaguely articulated and flexible expec-tations was that the suburban mothers tended to make a distinction between the child's 'wants' and the child's 'needs', even though the line was flexible and was often redrawn to cater for new circumstances. This distinction helped them to accommodate conflicting interests.

Carol, for example, told me how she was suffering from physical exhaustion when her baby was 9 months old. She was still breast-feeding him during the night, and 'somehow hadn't realized, look, he doesn't really need a feed during the night'. Making a distinction between needs and wants made it easier for Carol to be able to wean him from night feeds. In the alternative group, on the other hand, such a distinction could not, in general, have been made until the infant was much older.

Although the suburban mothers (and fathers) expressed aspirations for their child to grow up 'happy' and 'well-adjusted', they were guided more directly by their desire to have a 'good' child. 'Good' meant the child doing what it was told to do by the parent. 'Good' also meant acquiring social skills, such as sharing and learning ways of handling conflict with other children, such as taking turns.

Child-rearing ideals in the kinship group
The kinship group had much less formal contact with the child-centred literature. Only one mother had attended an ante-natal class, or read any literature on parenting before giving birth. In this smaller sample, three mothers had made no decision on how they were going to feed their child until after their baby was born. Nevertheless, the majority did breast-feed 'on demand' and only one tried to impose a feeding schedule onto the child.

Members of this group were also more pragmatic than the alternative mothers. They generally breast-fed on demand, but had little hesitation in switching to a bottle to allow their own mothers to feed their child when she offered to give them a break. During the first few months, however, most mothers in this group did try to understand the needs of their child from the child's point of view. Like the suburban mothers they worked out flexible and idiosyncratic routines with each of their children.

The kinship mothers also wanted their children to be 'good', couching their aspirations in moral rather than psychological terms. 'Good' for these mothers also meant the child doing what he or she was told to do by the parent. However, unlike the suburban mothers, the kinship mothers believed that all that was required of them to bring about a 'good' child was to correct their child after the event. Unlike the suburban mothers, they did not participate in their child's play so that they rarely intervened in the children's social activity. They did not make use of social situations to teach their child social skills. Instead, they chastised their child if a disturbance broke out and comforted their child if the child became upset.

Child-rearing ideals in the alternative group
Members of the alternative group were highly prepared for the birth of their child, having participated with their partners in ante-natal classes and read extensively on the psychological and spiritual development of children. They generally held firm expectations about what to expect from the birth and from themselves as mothers. All expected to breast-feed 'on demand' and were generally against mothering aids such as dummies and bottles, at least before their first child was born.

They articulated child-centred ideals very strongly, couching their aspirations for their children in psychological rather than moral terms. The emotional security of their children took precedence over every other need, and everyone else's interests. As one mother told me, her immediate concern was not to 'lay down really deep rooted emotional problems', and another, 'I just would never, ever, let her cry'.

The primary concern of the alternative mothers, then, was to lay down the foundations for their child's emotional security. Being more influenced than the other groups by child-rearing literature and psychological models of human development, they were acutely aware of potential mothering 'pathologies' that led to 'emotional hangups'. Their aspirations for the moral development of their children were secondary and expressed in terms of teaching their children to be 'socially responsible', rather than 'good', by which they meant they hoped that their children developed social attitudes that were environmentally sound and tolerant towards others.

In the next two chapters I describe how different maternal attitudes shape different patterns of maternal-infant interaction, which in turn structures different forms of subjectivity within children. In the rest of this chapter, I wish to address the more general question of the dynamics of the normative context of the three playgroups. How were the norms which shaped maternal attitudes 'enforced' by group members?

The dynamics of the normative context of playgroup

The interpersonal dependence of mothers

In all three playgroups, mothers depended considerably on the support they were given from other mothers in the group. They overwhelmingly expressed the need to discuss their child-rearing practices and maternal judgements with others 'in the same boat'. They needed to have their judgements confirmed. The 'enforcement' of group norms needs to be seen in this context of the mother's need for a supportive community of peers, since this need often took precedence over any individual mother's belief in the legitimacy of the content of the group's norms.

During playgroup, mothers would often seek an external criterion, or communal standard to assist them and confirm their judgement. A great many conversations in all groups turned on the minutiae of their concerns as mothers and primary carers and invited comment and support from other mothers. The playgroup environment provided them with this opportunity and the social standards against which to assess their work.

Kim's dilemma is illustrative. She arrived at playgroup one morning visibly upset and immediately started to talk to a group of mothers about it. Apparently she had trouble getting her older child to go to school and had negotiated an agreement whereby her daughter was happy to go so long as the mother stayed at school until the bell rang. However, she had just worked out an arrangement with her neighbour whereby they could share transport of the children to school. This morning it was her neighbour's turn to take the children, but her daughter had run away and hid. Eventually Kim had to take her own daughter to school.

None of the mothers in the group attempted to tell Kim how she *should* handle this situation. Instead, they offered her support with comments such as 'Lot's of children go through this'. They agreed with her, when she offered her own interpretation of the situation, that it was time that she took a firm stand on this issue with her daughter. This type of support, or confirmation, was particularly important to a mother who was still very ambiguous about what action to take.

In another example, a mother was discussing how difficult it was for her to wean her 14 month-old child with the mother next to her at the craft table. The child was at the stage of undoing her blouse in public and taking her breast out when he liked and she had 'just about enough'. It was hard for her though, even with this sort of harassment to just say no. His yelling was even more embarrassing than letting him have the breast. But even at home she said she found it hard to be consistent. Sometimes his cries would get to her and she would relent and other times she got so angry that she was able to say no.

The mother who was engaged with her in this conversation gave her support for both courses of action. She said first of all that she did not know how she could put up with it. She had managed to wean her baby over-night when the baby had bit her one day. But on the other hand, she also offered the mother the experience of a friend of hers who was still breast-feeding two of her children, but only as a nightcap. This had proved an expedient way of getting the children to go to bed.

The importance of having external standards to assist in making judgements and the confirmation that mothers sought from other mothers when making child-rearing decisions has been recognized as a 'need' by many Early Childhood Nurses who organize formal groups for this purpose. Chris told me what she got out of these meetings:

> We'd have little talks, you know, about issues to do with women's health and then afterwards we'd sort of linger around and we'd talk amongst ourselves about problems we were having with feeding, or when they got upset changing to solids, and you know, reassuring each other that our babies were normal and that we weren't, you know, bad mothers or anything like that.

The empathetic mechanism

The support that mothers obtained from other mothers operated through empathy. Mothers appeared to try to understand the situation of the other mother from the other mother's point of view by referring to their own experience. This was apparent in their anticipation of the needs of other mothers. For example, if a mother arrived at playgroup with a baby and toddler, someone usually went over to help her unload the car and watch out for the toddler.

Underlying the empathetic mechanism that operated in these groups was their shared experience of mothering and the task of giving primary care. They were also all vulnerable to the potential for their own child to sometimes be 'out of control'. More often that not, this helped guard against being too critical of other mothers. Because of their common vulnerability, they also took advantage of opportunities to strengthen the bonds that arose from these shared experiences, being prepared, for example to listen at length to a mother's birthing details and asking about feeding and sleeping problems.

These ties were evident when a new baby arrived. Other mothers would crowd around and smile and clutch the baby's fingers or touch the baby's cheek. They might even take it in turns to give the baby a cuddle and would often try to get their own children to show an interest in the new arrival.

The communal support and confirmation of child-rearing practices that the mothers and other female carers gave to each other was noticeably lacking for the fathers that I observed and interviewed. Even the fathers at playgroup, who were quite involved with parenting, did not participate in these exchanges. The regular attender of the suburban group often sat in the sun and read the paper. Another in the alternative group ended up going for a solitary walk each time he attended. A third who regularly attended the alternative group sat on the rug and talked to the mothers, but not about the minutiae of child-rearing. Unlike the mothers and female carers in my sample, the fathers that I interviewed all lacked a shared, communal experience of child-rearing.

This may be why child-rearing is so often portrayed as a 'private' activity, carried out within the confines of the isolated nuclear family. The communal activity that mothers and other carers in my sample participated in was very much the preserve of women. As women's activity its social dimension tends to remain obscured as does its impact on the process of socialization.[5] However, it is misleading to portray the constitution of maternal attitudes as something that occurs in a 'private' space. Maternal attitudes are not open to change simply through the potential of individual mothers to question their validity, since nurturing takes place within the context of the nurturer's need for a supportive community of peers.[6]

Empathy and the avoidance of group tension

Because of this need for a mutually supportive community of peers, 'fitting in' to the playgroup did not simply require that mothers 'know the rules', or the 'codes of conduct' of the playgroup. Mothers also had to adopt the appropriate attitude toward other mothers in the group. This attitude depended upon the mother possessing a certain interactive competence to empathize with other mothers. In part, this competence was derived from their shared experience of mothering.

The empathetic mechanism that allowed mothers to support each other in their child-rearing activity also helps to explain how the relationships in the group were maintained, in that an empathetic attitude facilitated the anticipation and avoidance of situations that might produce tension within the group. When I asked the mothers during interviews why they did not chastise another mother's child, the general reply was because they would not like it if someone chastised *their* child. Lyn, for example, expressed the view that it would cause too much tension in the group if they did and told me about an incident last year in which another mother 'abused' her little girl and made her little girl cry. Lyn got angry with the mother because she felt it had been unfair. The mother got up and 'stormed off' and never came back to playgroup.

The guiding factor behind mothers conforming to this norm was the desire on their behalf to avoid such a confrontation. Mothers anticipated conflict within the group and acted to avoid any confrontation as far as practicable. This involved mothers in an empathetic process of understanding the perspective of other mothers, and making subtle changes in their own behaviour to accommodate the interests of others.

This also meant that the norms of the group depended very much upon the particular mothers and carers who were present. Who was present determined social behaviour to a significant extent, since subtle changes in behaviour often occurred, depending on who was in the group at the time. However, parents that I interviewed were acutely aware of how differently they felt and behaved towards their children according to whom they happened to be with in *all* social situations, not only in playgroup.

To illustrate, when I asked Lyn if she behaved differently towards her child in different social situations she replied:

> Oh, it has to be different I think. I mean, you're putting on a performance aren't you, depending on who's around . . . People you see all the time, it doesn't worry you. If I was at, say, Andrew's [her husband's] parents' place I would have a certain way I would chastise the children. You know, at mum's place it would be different again because I'm more at home at mum's place than when I'm at Andrew's mum's place.

Three fathers also mentioned being affected differently by the particularities of the people that were present. John, a 'role swap' father said:

> Actually, it's really weird. I had to smack Jody a few times, well, when I say smack her I don't think I've ever physically hurt her. But I've smacked her when other people have been around mainly because I have thought that was what I was expected to do. Whereas at home I wouldn't do that. Yes, I think other people around can

influence me. If it's people I'm really close to, no, it's not going to bother me . . .

The need to accommodate other perspectives was not experienced so acutely by the kinship mothers. The kinship mothers did not generally reply to this line of questioning by discussing how differently they acted towards their children in different social situations. I suggest that this was because they were not exposed to the diverse social situations that the suburban and alternative mothers were exposed to. Their playgroup and immediate social environment was close knit, or 'traditional'. There simply was not the same diversity of perspectives that confronted mothers, particularly in the suburban group, and their seemingly constant need to anticipate different expectations.

The normative context of communal forms of social organization

My discussion of the moral dimension of communal forms of social organization in Chapter 2, helps to draw out the dynamics of the playgroup normative context. The social sphere in which nurturing is carried out is constrained by the overriding need for the mothers involved to maintain the relationships within the group. Action, particularly the supportive and interpretive action of the mothers, is often an end in itself, in that it maintains these relationships. However, action is not only guided by the need to maintain relationships. It is also, in part, directed by ideals and considered ends. Child-rearing ideals play an important part in constructing maternal attitudes and these *are* open to discursive argumentation and change.

Mothers are also very much involved in articulating the concerns that arise from mothering practices and they express judgements about social practices that impact on these concerns. Conversations at playgroup often brought up 'public' issues, such as the lack of social planning for mothers and children in new housing estates, the way shopping centres added to their frustrations, the problems with the hospital system, their treatment by employers, etc. Gender roles were also often under review, with mothers comparing notes about how much their respective spouses contributed to domestic labour! But the suburban and alternative mothers had much more opportunity to question gendered expectations, since they were confronted by far more diversity of life experience than the kinship mothers. I suggest that diversity plays an important part in the potential for people to question traditional expectations and seek change.

Thus, even though playgroups primarily have a communal orientation, they also have the potential to enable mothers to articulate their common concerns and question their current way of doing things. While they need to make reference to their socio-cultural milieu to make their nurturing judgements, they also have the opportunity to question the social practices they find there and the value systems which sustain them. The suburban and alternative groups also demonstrated that when groups of mothers get together they can utilize the organization of associative structures to bring their concerns as mothers into the public world.

Although I have focused on the positive aspect of the affective ties that exist within playgroup, there is also a negative side to these ties which helps to explain the dynamic nature of communal forms of social organization. Negative affects are often elicited in mothers during playgroup. As I mentioned briefly in this chapter, mothers may experience a great deal of emotional discomfit, or shame, particularly when their child is outside of their control. On the one hand, then, the empathetic mechanism gives mothers emotional support and confirmation of their maternal judgements, but on the other hand, these same ties expose the mother to potentially stressful situations. Mothers are, in fact, often shamed by their child's behaviour. It is this experience of shame that reinforces the mother's experience of herself as being personally responsible for her own child's behaviour. For most mothers, it is this experience of shame that then leads them to intervene in their child's activity. However, for a number of mothers, the experience of shame is intense and frequent and may lead to a loss of self-esteem when they perceive themselves as failing to live up to the expected standards.

6 // Taking the attitude of the child

The agency of the child

In all three playgroups, it was strikingly obvious that young children exert considerable influence over the actions of their mothers. They are often able to assert their interests over the immediate interests of their mothers. This ability to affect the actions of the mother was most obvious in the way that mothers also felt distressed when their child appeared to be distressed and acted to avoid their infant's distress even if this meant inconveniencing themselves to a considerable degree. It was particularly apparent in the case of mothers who had prior expectations that they would not be affected.

For example, there were a few mothers who expected to be able to impose their own schedule, or daily routine, onto their child. They wanted their child to simply fit in with their existing lifestyle. However, they experienced great difficulty when they attempted to do this and had to modify their own daily routines to fit in with the child.

Sandra, for example, had decided to bottle-feed her infant every four hours, expecting that the infant would simply sleep and eat at the appropriate times. When I asked her what she did, then, when the baby cried between feeds, she replied:

> Tried to pacify him. I'd be out at 6 o'clock in the morning pushing this pram around the streets. It was lucky it was summer. I'd walk for miles and miles.

Jan's expectations were largely shaped by her husband who wanted the child to fit in immediately with the regime he had worked out. Jan was to feed the child 'by the clock' and her husband attempted to ensure that Jan followed his rules. However, ignoring her child when the child was crying produced a great deal of anxiety in Jan which did not appear to be the case with either her husband or the nursing staff that assisted her when she was sick and confined to bed:

> When I used to hear her cry it would really upset me because I wanted to get out [of bed] and grab her or do something. There were times when the doctors wouldn't even let me pick her up . . . And like if she fell over and my mother-in-law or my husband or whoever was looking after her was out of the room, I would just pick her up. I just couldn't help it, you know. I wouldn't have been able to not do it.

Infant research has described how mothers come to anticipate crying and respond before the crying becomes too intense. Bell (1974) has referred to this mode of interaction as 'homeostatic' implying that a balance is achieved. Using video-tapes of maternal-infant interaction, Bell (p. 4) describes how the mother's response to the early items in a sequence averts a later item. Brazelton (1974) has elaborated further on Bell's 1974 model, describing how mothers set up an 'expectancy of interaction' (p. 73) which involves the mother learning the child's limits.

However, in this research it is assumed that the child's assertiveness is expressed and institutionalized in the same way in all dyads. This was not the case in my study. It was predominantly in the suburban group, where the mother took the attitude of the child on a continuing basis, that the mother built up a perspective of her child and learnt to antici-pate distress and possible sources of confrontation. In the kinship and alternative groups there was a greater predominance of subject-object relations. In the kinship group, this led to the child's assertiveness being expressed in acts of resistance and defiance, and in the alternative group, it led to the mother organizing her life almost totally around the demands of the child.

The anticipation of confrontation: 'following behaviour'

By taking the attitude of the child, the mothers in the suburban group were more clearly able to distinguish two perspectives and coordinate these through a process of understanding. The mother was prepared to inconvenience herself somewhat, but within certain limits that were arrived at through weighing up competing demands. Nevertheless, there were also absolute limits set by the child, which the mother had to come to recognize and accommodate if she was to demonstrate the appropriate maternal attitude of the group.

The child's absolute limits became incorporated into the mother's per-spective of her own particular child that she built up over time. The outcome of this process of understanding and incorporation could be observed in a number of interactive patterns, or rituals, which were built up from the mother's anticipation and avoidance of the child's limits.

'Following behaviour' is an example of a ritual that institutionalized the assertiveness of the child. It demonstrates a pattern of interaction in which the mother[1] anticipates the limits of her child and acts to avoid the confrontation that would ensue if the child had to assert this limit. A confrontation might provoke an uncontrollable episode of crying or screaming from the child and prove embarrassing for the mother in front of the other members of the group. It is within the context of this *group* approval of the appropriate maternal attitude that the child was able to assert his or her own set of interests.

Rhonda, for example, is a mother I refer to as 'a prompt follower', relatively common in the suburban group. Rhonda was a psychology graduate and very child-centred. Whenever Rhonda would sit down to talk, her daughter, Julie, would run up and take her hand, tugging at her to follow. Rhonda would cut the conversation short and allow herself to be tugged away to watch Julie play. Mothers who were forced to disrupt their conversation to allow another mother to follow her child, gave a sympathetic nod, or shrug which gave the mother following her child the message that this was just to be expected.

It was sometimes possible for a mother to delay following and continue with her own activity by distracting the child. These 'delaying tactics' that mothers used demonstrated the presence of the mother's own set of interests that were sometimes in conflict with the child's immediate interests. Yet, many mothers were prepared to allow the child to assert themselves here. For example, while I was talking to a mother beside the sandpit, her 2 year-old daughter came up and began tugging at her arm. The mother was quite intent to finish the conversation, however, and I noticed that she began stroking her daughter and playing with her daughter's hand. Then she lifted her daughter, struggling, up onto her knee. But when the struggling failed to abate, the mother got up and followed her child.

There were mothers in the suburban group who were not as prompt at following as Rhonda. When they were less prompt, it was easier to observe the two sets of interests which the mother was considering. I identified 'reluctant following' to depict situations in which this conflict was apparent and eventually resolved by the assertiveness of the child, whose power was enhanced by the context of the more child-centred suburban group. In these cases, mothers would generally be engaged in conversation with other mothers and be reluctant to break off from their own activity to attend to their child. They would usually attempt to avoid having to leave the group by pointing and gesticulating and giving verbal instructions to their child. However, after continued tugging, the mother would leave her friends and follow her child. It seemed apparent to me that these reluctant followers were well aware of the expectations in the group that the mother should avoid a direct confrontation with her child if at all possible, even if this meant 'giving in' on the matter of following.

On the other hand, in the kinship group 'following behaviour' was not ritualized. In fact, it seemed to be actively discouraged. For example, I noticed one morning in the kinship playgroup that Mary's little girl was tugging at her hand, wanting her mother to go outside with her. I had been watching the child being bullied in the outside play area through the window and knew that the child wanted the mother to come out into the yard to protect her. Mary, who was aware of the situation in the yard, seemed to want to follow. She made as if to stand up and go a few times, but then sat down, looking around at the other mothers. The core group of mothers had often expressed the view that children should be left to sort out their own problems. Since no mothers supervised their children in the yard as a matter of course, it did not seem to be appropriate for a mother to allow her child to drag her away from the other mothers. Nevertheless, when I stood up to go outside a short while later, Mary immediately got up and came outside with me.

I suggest that the reason the kinship mothers did not feel compelled to follow their child may be related to the fact that the kinship mothers also felt less embarrassment when their children were distressed, or misbehaved in public. This was also reflected in the fact that there was no group norm which expected mothers to actively supervise their children in the play area.

'Following behaviour' was expressed differently in the alternative group. The children in this group tended to simply wander away. They did not usually try to get their mothers to follow, since these children were not in any immediate need for their mother's protection against other children. The alternative mothers found this somewhat annoying, but they never attempted to coerce a child to return. They might call to the child to come back, or try to entice them back with the offer of something to eat but if this failed, at least one of the mothers would offer to follow while the remaining mothers kept an eye on the babies on the rug. The children in the alternative group therefore experienced tremendous freedom, relative to the children in the other two groups, but only rarely had to confront and deal with conflict with other children.[2]

The anticipation and avoidance of the child's distress

In the suburban group, the assertiveness of the child also became institutionalized in ritualized patterns of behaviour which enabled mothers to anticipate and avoid potentially distressing situations for their child. These rituals were so effective that I only began to realize they existed when they failed to occur. I was then able to observe the ritual more closely and note the differences in each group.

'Arrival behaviour' is an example of one such ritual. On arrival at the suburban playgroup, most mothers[3] would find somewhere for their child to play and sit down with them at the play station. They would sometimes get involved in the play activity with their child, or at least sit close to the child until the child began to take part in the activity. When the child was happily playing, the mother might then move away to talk to a friend, or sign the attendance book.

My attention was drawn to 'arrival behaviour' one morning when Sandra arrived with her two children, Jamie 3 years and Ben 12 months. She placed Ben on the floor in the shed and then paused for a moment, before moving away to sign the attendance book. Her pause drew my attention and I realized, as did the mother, that she had moved away too soon. The child began to cry and the mother was back in a matter of seconds. She picked the baby up and placed him on her hip, where he remained for most of the morning while Sandra followed Jamie around the yard.

On the other hand, mothers in the kinship group had not ritualized 'arrival behaviour' in this way. Children were expected to go outside and play unaccompanied by their mother or carer. If the child became distressed, he or she was picked up and cuddled, but put down as soon as the crying abated. The child would start crying again and the pattern would repeat itself. Mothers here did not attempt to settle their child down in *anticipation* of the child's distress, nor did they appear to try to work out why the child was distressed.

The 'arrival behaviour' of the alternative group differed to the extent that the mothers settled themselves down comfortably and allowed the children to remain on their laps and at their breasts for as long as they liked. The children tended to stay very close to their mothers, or to the carer who was looking after them for the morning, when they first arrived. They gradually moved away from their mothers or carers to explore their surroundings, frequently returning to sit on their mother's knee or close to their carer.

When mothers do not take the attitude of the child and anticipate and avoid confrontation and potentially distressing situations for the child, subject-object relations become the dominant mode of interaction. As we shall see in the next chapter, subject-object relations are an important dimension of all parent–child relations. However, in the absence of a primary carer adopting the attitude of the child, the child's assertiveness becomes patterned into modes of relating to others that exhibit resistance and manipulation, rather than self-assertiveness and concern for another.

Constituting meanings through the negotiation of interests
In all three groups, the assertiveness of the child was also apparent in the way in which ideals came to be redefined in the course of child-rearing. The shifts in meaning that occurred were the result of the mother's need to accommodate the agency of the child, in a child-centred, normative context. This was most apparent in the way in which previously held expectations and child-rearing ideals had to be modified during the early child-rearing period.

The most striking example was the way in which 'demand feeding' came to be defined. 'Demand feeding' refers to the currently popular way of feeding infants. Consistent with current child-rearing trends, this method of feeding implies that the mother should try to fit in with the pattern of demand for food that is dictated by the child. I soon discovered, however, that this ideal was open to a wide range of interpretations, depending upon the outcome of the negotiation process.

The meaning of demand feeding came to reflect whatever rationalization the mother found necessary to accommodate the results of her negotiation efforts. It could mean anything from giving the infant the breast every time the baby became agitated or cried, to giving the child a feed as a last resort, when all other means of pacifying the infant had failed.

This latter interpretation was the most common, since it gave the mother far more scope for introducing a variety of other responses that could eventually be taken over by other carers. Karen, for example, claimed that she demand fed her baby, but she was clearly keen to have other adults care for her child as much as possible. She was usually accompanied at playgroup by her neighbour, Margaret, who had no children of her own but who enjoyed helping Karen care for her children.

One morning, Margaret was sitting with a group of mothers, nursing Karen's baby on her knee. The baby started whimpering and Margaret began to get agitated. The crying became louder and Margaret stood up. 'What should I do?' Margaret asked the group. 'Try walking around a bit,' I replied in the absence of any other suggestions. 'Do you want him?' Margaret asked the mother. 'No,' said the mother, 'he's not hungry because I just fed him.' 'How are you feeding him?' I asked his mother. 'Bottle,' said Karen, 'but on demand.'

'On demand' for Karen meant giving her baby food when she thought he should be hungry, rather than pacifying him with food every time he cried. Karen had apparently worked out this definition of demand feeding very early in their relationship. It gave her far greater scope to accommodate her own interests. Robyn began child-rearing expecting to demand feed according to the wisdom gained from her nursing training. She was determined to demand feed because she strongly believed that demand feeding was in the best interests of the child. She initially thought that demand feeding meant putting the infant to the breast every time the infant cried. However, she soon became aware of a conflict between this interpretation of the ideal and her own set of interests. Robyn had to modify her interpretation of this ideal in order to accommodate her own interests:

Well, I started off demand [feeding]. I thought, this is ridiculous, every hour . . . She just wanted the breast for comfort, which was very straining on me, very, you can't have 2 minutes to yourself. It's very hard. And so I got the old dummy out. And that was marvellous.

Kathy breast-fed her first child 'on demand', meaning every time the infant would accept the breast. Her first baby had been premature and Kathy was concerned to give the baby as much food as possible. However, with the second baby Kathy intended to return to work soon after the birth. Her great concern this time was to get the baby into a routine for someone else to look after. 'Demand feeding' became only feeding him when Kathy thought he really needed to eat. His cries did not affect her as much as her first child's, because she believed that she had no alternative but to let him cry. She was able to modify her interpretation of the demand feeding ideal to fit in with the pragmatic requirements of her life:

> I was quite happy to let him cry. Because he was fighting the breast and wanted a bottle. And he was wanting to be fed constantly. So it was very easy to let him cry. But he wasn't premmy and he was really strong . . . I knew he was putting on weight something shocking . . . over a pound a week. And that was a lot . . . So with Kim running around and going to work and everything, so, [I thought] you'll cope. You're getting fed when you're supposed to be fed . . . and we only had 5 weeks to get him into a routine.

When Kathy went back to work after five weeks, the father of the child took over as primary carer. They both worked shift work to allow one of them to care for their children. It is significant, I believe, that the mother still felt that she was the one who had to get the new baby into a routine before she felt comfortable leaving him, even though she was to leave him with the father who in Kathy's opinion was a better 'mother' than her anyway.

The negotiation of two sets of interests could be seen in other caregiving tasks, besides feeding, which gave rise to the necessity to redefine previously held child-rearing ideals. Sue, for example, told me how she changed many of the ideas she got from ante-natal classes when these clashed too severely with her own interests:

> Like, people would tell me not to use a walker, but O.K. fair enough if you leave them in there for twenty-four hours a day, it's no good. But if you put them in there for an hour when you're in the kitchen cooking they love it. So I changed all those ideas, all those. Because pre-natal classes taught me don't do this . . . they were really funny actually. They try and make you against anything like that [bottles, dummies, walkers and other care-giving aids].

The confrontation between child-centred ideals and the mother's own interests may not become apparent with a 'good' baby who is easily pacified and fits in with the parents' lifestyle. However, re-defining ideals might occur with a subsequent baby who is more demanding. An alternative mother, Rebecca, told me how her first baby just fitted in with her life, but the second required her to make some adjustments. She had to modify her understanding of demand feeding, in order to accommodate the very great demands of her second child. Because she adhered so strongly to her ideals, her need to eventually impose some limits on her infant's demands was very emotionally draining and traumatic for her. Rebecca solved this problem by admitting that her infant was particularly demanding and did not really need to be fed all the times she appeared to want to feed. In order to retain a positive image of her child, she redefined what she thought a 'good' baby entailed. In her reinterpretation, a 'good' baby became a 'super perceptive' baby:

> I think crying babies like that are really just a bit freaked out because they're sensitive . . . you know, very intuitive. If there's something going on, like if I have a bit of a fight with [the father] or something, she picks up on it straight away. She knows all those sorts of things. I think she's really on that level. And as a baby she was probably super perceptive.

Demand feeding in the context of professional advice

Mothers in both the suburban and kinship groups were very much influenced by the infant care literature on demand feeding. While mothers did find room within this concept to accommodate their own interests, according to their own particular situations, the notion itself has been very influential in shaping the maternal attitude orientated towards understanding. The shift in infant care patterns from the 'scheduling' to the demand feeding, or 'natural' approach, is in fact a shift towards a more child-centred approach to nurturing, in that trying to find out exactly what the infant wants often leads to an intense preoccupation on the part of the mother with the infant's slightest actions. The predominance of the maternal attitude orientated towards understanding in early infant care should be seen in the context of this shift and the role of professional discourse on infant care.

The dominance of this attitude is nowhere more apparent than in the general acceptance of the notion of 'demand feeding', even by the kinship mothers who were still also greatly influenced by the infant care patterns of their own mothers. The infant care advice given out in hospitals and by the early childhood nurses has been very effective in its objective.

However, the early childhood nurses working from the baby health clinics attended by the suburban and kinship mothers, tended to offer advice to mothers pragmatically, in a supportive rather than dogmatic manner.[4] Their attitude was reflected in the more pragmatic attitude to mothering taken by mothers in these two groups. Mothers in these two groups accommodated their infant's demands by weighing up their own concerns and the interests of other family members. However, a very different picture emerged from the alternative group, who generally rejected both their own mothers' way of doing things and the mainstream advice given out in baby health centres.

These mothers were more directly influenced by themes derived from psychological theories. The most important theme was the need to gratify all the infant's 'needs' to ensure an emotionally secure, and self-assertive individual. Another theme was that of fostering creativity and spontaneity in their children. This meant trying not to impose any structure on the child, in the belief that this would hamper the child's spontaneity and creativity and the development of the child's individuality. Their interpretation of demand-feeding needs to be seen in this light, heavily influenced by the 1960s anti-structure, back-to-nature rhetoric, and unmediated by the pragmatism of early childhood nurses.

Josie, for example, believed that fitting in with all the demands of the child would ensure a very secure and self-assertive child. Like most of the alternative mothers, she interpreted every demand as a need for the breast. Demand feeding for Josie meant giving the baby the breast every time the baby became agitated, or cried. No routine, or care-giving pattern emerged that allowed Josie time off from caring for her baby, but Josie was prepared to accept this outcome, even though this meant she was often physically exhausted.

The emergence of daily routines

Idiosyncratic care-giving patterns emerged within each dyad in the suburban and kinship groups which demonstrated compromise solutions to conflicts of interest that arose between the mother and child. These patterns were the negotiated outcome of the mother's attempts to coordinate her own set of interests with those of the child. As a result, care-giving became crystallized into a more or less predictable daily routine that allowed mothers some degree of personal autonomy, while also allowing input from the child.

When patterns emerged, mothers could predict the needs of her own particular child to some extent and could then allocate care-giving tasks to others, or focus on some other activity knowing that their child would not require 'close attention giving' for that period of time. The psychological literature has also observed the way in which many mothers manage to achieve some predictability in their care-giving patterns, while allowing for the agency of the child. Kaye's study, for example, describes the 'jiggling actions' of mothers with their newborns as an attempt by them to find some regularity, or predictability, in their interaction which was not based on the clock as in the old scheduling days but on 'mutual monitoring and feedback' (Schaffer and Dunn 1979: 27).

While most of the alternative group tried to avoid imposing any structure on their child and were prepared to live with the unpredictability of the demands of their children, the vast majority of mothers in both the suburban and kinship groups did achieve some regularity in their care-giving activity through the 'mutual monitoring and feedback' that comprised the negotiation process. The patterns which emerged, however, were also flexible and subject to change at the instigation of either party. As Lorraine, a kinship mother described it:

> Andrew would have been about three months old. He'd have about 5 feeds a day and then he started cutting down. Because he used to have a feed at 11 o'clock in the morning and then he cut that out, he wouldn't have it until lunch time ... [the next child] was more or less the same as Andrew. Little bit different though. Like you'd get her into one routine and she'd turn around and change it again every two weeks or so. You'd get into it, and she'd change it all around again ... she'd wake up at different times. Different times she'd want a feed.

In the suburban group, these patterns continued on throughout the child's early life. Rhonda's description of her bed-time ritual with her child demonstrates the way in which compromise solutions were achieved by mothers:

> She refuses to go to sleep during the day, and at night time we've got into a pattern of we have a bath and we hop into bed and we have a nice sort of ritual ... [bottle, stories, songs and prayer time] ... and she's ready to go to sleep then, but we usually have, 'oh well, mummy's got to go to bed with me in her bed' struggle, about once or twice a week now, which is fine because you just say, No and walk out and she cries for two minutes and then forgets about it and goes to sleep, so that's nice.

In the alternative group, however, mothers tended to give their infants the breast in response to all demands on the part of the child. No routines emerged that allowed the mother to feel comfortable about leaving their child with another carer. Routines were generally considered to be an imposition on the child, so that the mothers tended to have to organize their life around caring for their child.

The mutual construction of subjectivity

I have used the concept 'taking the attitude of the child' with the deliberate intention of stressing the fact that care-giving within a singular care-giving relationship involves a *mutual* internalization process. In other words, there is an embodied, structuring effect within the nurturer as well as within the child. The child's bodily drives are structured as 'needs' through the interpretive efforts of the nurturer, but in the process, the nurturer's physiology also becomes patterned. I suggest that it is the 'imprinting', or development of these patterns, that largely explains the different attitude of the early primary care-giver compared to subsequent care-givers.

It is significant, therefore, that it is primarily the mother who nurtures, in the context of the intense normative pressure that now exists for children's 'needs' to be immediately gratified. In the process of interpreting and structuring the infant's actions as 'needs', the mother's own body is also subjected to an internal, structuring effect. In other words, the patterns of communication which develop between the mother and child become embodied in both the mother and the child.

Kohut (1983) uses the term 'neuro-physiological psychological configurations' to depict the structuring of the self. As Kohut's terminology suggests, the child's subjectivity consists of the internal patterning effect of the child's neuro-physiological system. However, what I have tried to show is that it is not just the gratifying, or frustrating of the child's bodily drives that is central here, but the 'knowing' process itself. The child's physiology becomes patterned, or structured, in response to the interpretive efforts of the mother. This process is socially constructed and socially constrained.

Moreover, by using an intersubjective action scheme it is possible to see that the neuro-physiological psychological configurations that are laid down in the child as a result of early maternal-infant interaction have their counterpart in the inner structuring of the mother's neuro-physiological system. The early period of nurturing, within the dominant child-centred context, largely determines the mother's future orientation or attitude towards her child's care.

The distinctive orientation of the mother to her child becomes more apparent as the singular care-giving relationship develops, particularly if the mother is breast-feeding 'on demand'. In this case, breast-feeding does not simply involve the mother in the instrumental act of giving food to the child. A breast-feeding mother may also use the breast to help her determine what the infant's 'needs' are. The breast may become a means of comfort, a way of consoling the child if the child becomes agitated. The mother's acceptance of the responsibility for primary care comes, at least in part, from her belief that she *is* the only one who can satisfy the child.

However, child-rearing ideals also play an important part in breast-feeding practices. The breast was used as a source of comfort far more often in mothers who perceived every agitated action of the infant as a need that had to be gratified. As we have seen, the alternative mothers in particular held a strong moral commitment to this child-rearing ideal. They tended to interpret all the infant's cries as a need for the breast, at least in the early stages, and felt strongly that all infant's needs should be satisfied if the infant was to develop into a secure adult.

The decision to breast-feed 'on demand' places the mother in the position of accepting the primary responsibility for *defining* the infant's 'needs', as well as gratifying them. By accepting the current breast-feeding wisdom, which recommends feeding as often as possible and whenever the infant appears to want a feed, mothers are placed in the position of making judgements as to what the child really does want.[5]

However, even the mothers who bottle-fed their infants according to a schedule adopted an orientation towards understanding their newborns. That is, they still attempted to understand the needs of their own particular child. Because they 'knew' their child 'couldn't be hungry' they tended to look for other explanations for their infant's crying. Sharon, for example, concluded that her child 'had trouble sleeping'. Instead of putting him to the breast when he cried, Sharon put her infant in a pram and took him for long walks.

As a result of taking the attitude of the child, the mother builds up a perspective of her own particular child which she uses to make judgements about future needs. As this process of understanding develops, the mother begins to anticipate her child's needs accordingly. Taking the attitude of the child thus helps the mother to anticipate the distress of her child and avoid unnecessary tension. Anticipating distress and avoiding conflict are important in the more child-centred, normative contexts. The need to avoid the infant's distress and conflict situations motivates mothers to continue to adopt this orientation towards understanding. However, this interactive pattern tended not to persist in the kinship group after the infants had settled down into a fairly predictable routine.

Resistance and defiance in the kinship group

Mothers in all groups sometimes failed to anticipate and avoid distress and confrontation and isolated acts of resistance and defiance also occurred in all groups. There were also individual cases in the suburban group where subject-object relations were more predominant. I shall refer to these in more detail in the next chapter. However, in the kinship group, coercion appeared to be the *expected* mode of directing the child's activity.

Patterns of interaction demonstrated acts of resistance and defiance, manipulation and coercion more than understanding. For example, children would react to the distress caused by being left to fend for themselves in the play area by clinging to their mothers and refusing to let go. This pattern repeated itself with regard to Sandra and her son, Ted, every morning I attended the playgroup. Sandra would sometimes try to push Ted away to go and play, but the more she pushed the harder Ted would cling to her. Once Ted bit Sandra on the leg. Sandra responded to this with a hard smack, but when Ted cried, Sandra picked him up and cuddled him tightly.

There was no active supervision in the yard, but any mother whose child was misbehaving was expected to go outside and bring the behaviour of her child under control. There was one 3 year-old boy, Tim, who went from one anti-social act to another. His mother, Lyn, spent most of her time at playgroup following him around the play area chastising him. When Tim became sufficiently annoyed at his mother's constant admonishments, he would indulge in defiant acts towards his mother, such as deliberately throwing toys over the fence, or pulling off the palings from the fence.

My experience with the kinship group made me aware that it is possible for a child to affect the mother, without the mother necessarily engaging in the intensive efforts to understand the child's perspective that I had witnessed in the suburban group, which was more child-centred. Explanations for anti-social behaviour may be given after the event, which leave the mother blameless, but these do not seem to be the result of attempting to understand the child from the child's point of view and they are not anticipated. The child is simply said to be 'hyper-active' or perhaps 'sooky today', meaning especially demanding of the mother's attention.

It appeared to me that in the kinship group intense confrontations with children were more acceptable and they certainly occurred more frequently. Since there was no norm, or social expectation that mothers should be involved in the children's activities, and mothers did not feel under any pressure to use the opportunity afforded by the playgroup to teach their children social skills, there was no real need for the mothers to construct a perspective of the child. Thus, the dyad's interaction in this group tended to be guided strategically.

Since they did not make the intensive effort to understand their child's perspective, they had not built up patterns of interaction based on understanding to the extent that the suburban mothers had. Like mothers in all the groups, the kinship mothers wanted their children to do what they were told. But the mothers in the kinship group seemed to believe that this would occur simply through coercion. There was more vehement disapproval expressed about children's anti-social behaviour and they were also far more likely than the other two groups to believe that, for example, biting a child back ('hard or it has no effect'), or giving them a good hiding was what was required. Lacking a well-developed perspective of their child that they could draw on to anticipate their child's needs and avoid confrontation, they had to rely far more on coercive methods of control. The social relations that existed between them were more frequently directly manipulative, or subject-object. The child's subjectivity was being built up on the basis of this relation of domination and submission.

The avoidance of confrontation in the alternative group
The alternative mothers provided a stark contrast to the kinship mothers. Feeling angry with a child was generally experienced by these mothers as their own failing. They felt the need to account for their 'negative feelings' towards their children in terms of how tired they were, or how they had just 'reached their limit' and 'lost control'. These mothers went to great lengths to avoid any confrontation, between themselves and

their children and between other children. Their meetings were consciously planned to keep potential disputes between the children to a minimum. The alternative mothers perceived their own interests to be whatever was in the interests of the child. Two sets of interests were not clearly defined during the early stages of child-rearing, since the mothers were generally willing to organize their lives around their child's demands. Conflict was therefore minimized, and the two perspectives not clearly differentiated. Action tended to be coordinated by the mother organizing her life, day and night, around the demands of her child.

This meant that in general no care-giving routines emerged which allowed the mother to predict to some degree the needs of her child. This made it very difficult for alternative mothers to leave their children for any length of time. When Rebecca arrived at my house for our interview, she had left her two children alone with the father for the very first time. She told me how anxious she felt leaving the children, even though she knew the father was quite capable of caring for them.

Ultimately, however, the mother would reach her limit. For the alternative mothers, this was delayed as long as possible. The crunch tended to come when the mother was simply too exhausted to continue feeding the child during the night and decided to wean the child. Weaning is often a problem for the mother, but in the case of the alternative mothers who had tried for so long to avoid any direct confrontation with their child, weaning was particularly traumatic. It enraged the child and exhausted the mother.

There were three alternative mothers who were going through an intense and exhausting period of weaning while I was involved with the group. Their descriptions of this experience were remarkably similar to the account given by Mary Ainsworth (1977a) of weaning behaviour in Ganda. According to Ainsworth, Gandan infants are given the breast for every discomfort and (like the alternative infants) eventually come to take the initiative and pacify themselves by helping themselves to the breast.

Ainsworth compares this to her sample of American mothers, where feeding behaviour 'splinters off' from other attachment behaviours. Since feeding becomes differentiated from comfort, feeding behaviour does not become integrated into the attachment relationship. Weaning does not prove to be so traumatic for the child, since the attachment relationship is not threatened. In the Gandan sample, on the other hand, feeding behaviour becomes so enmeshed in the organization of the attachment relationship that weaning may threaten the whole relationship.

While the children of the alternative mothers certainly did not appear to be suffering unduly from their mother's attentions, their considerable freedom was gained at the expense of the mother's freedom. The alternative mothers were prepared to forgo this freedom, at least in the short term. Since conflict situations were ultimately unavoidable, these children were also eventually forced to deal with conflict with their mothers, as we shall see more clearly in the next chapter.

7 // Maternal attitudes and maternal-infant conflict

Disciplinary action

I have described the social relations which underlie maternal attitudes as shifting between subject-object and subject-subject. Subject-object relations operate when either the mother or child attempts to set an absolute limit on the other. There is at this point no space for negotiation. In the last chapter, I described how the assertiveness of the child became expressed and institutionalized in the interactive patterns of the dyad. What happens, then, when the mother is dominant, that is, when the mother sets an absolute limit which is not negotiable?[1]

In these confrontations, the mother is quite obviously attempting to direct the child's actions. How does this subject-object social relation, in which the mother is dominant, relate to the underlying orientation towards understanding? Do different maternal attitudes make a difference to the outcome of maternal-infant conflict? I developed the concept of a 'reparative discipline cycle' to address these questions.

A reparative discipline cycle

A reparative discipline cycle begins with the mother asserting a definite social boundary in which there is absolutely no space for negotiation. This situation is provoked by the feeling of personal responsibility for the child's social behaviour. An anti-social act performed by the child elicits in the mother a feeling of shame, which often gives way to anger, or at least some expression of withdrawal from the child.

The immediate social relation involved in this highly emotional exchange is subject-object. The mother is intent on directing the child's social behaviour. In the study, the outcome of this emotional exchange of hostility differed according to the predominant maternal attitude.

The suburban group

The reparative discipline cycle emerged most clearly in the suburban group, where the mother's predominant orientation was towards understanding. Disciplinary action taken by the mother could be seen as cyclical, rather than linear, in that the social relations of mother and child passed through moments of subject-object dominance and became restored to a subject-subject relation in a mutual healing process.

I observed an example of this cycle one morning in the suburban group after a mother smacked her 3 year-old daughter, Beth, for 'gouging' a younger girl's face. Beth had thrown herself to the ground and was crying loudly. The mother sat with a group of other mothers, apparently unmoved by her daughter's state, although she still appeared to be angry. A short time later, Beth's brother and cousin came up and began to 'pat' Beth with the pretence of consoling her. The 'pats' got harder and rougher until Beth was in such a state of distress that her mother went over and picked her up, verbally castigating the boys for being so rough. She sat down with Beth on her knee and they cuddled. After a short time, the mother got up and went out to the car for Beth's bottle, which she kept for Beth as a special treat. She lifted Beth back up onto her knee and cuddled her again as she fed Beth the bottle.

The crucial feature of the reparative discipline cycle is the child's experience of distress, following the withdrawal of the mother's love. The child's experience of distress ultimately effects the mother as well the child, so that both the mother and child become orientated towards reconciling their relationship. During the period of reconciliation the bond between the mother and child appears to strengthen. Thus, this cycle of emotionally intense interaction lays down new neuro-physiological pathways that develop into new psychological configurations in *both* the mother and child.[2]

A confrontation between the mother and child might lead, in the first instance, to the child becoming very angry, or enraged, with the mother. The usual response is for the mother to wait until the child's rage abates, ignoring the child's behaviour as far as possible. Eventually the child feels her withdrawal and wants to be comforted. As in the example above, a period of reconciliation, or healing, follows.

For example, one morning in the suburban group, I watched Sharon trying to defuse a conflict that had reared up between her 3 year-old daughter, Amy, and another little girl over some playdough toys. Sharon tried first of all to get Amy to play outside. When Amy refused and continued to scream at the little girl, Sharon walked outside on her own, leaving her daughter in the shed. Amy came screaming out after her mother and tugged at her, trying to get her to go back inside the shed with her. Sharon stood her ground and Amy began to hit her mother and then threw herself on the ground. Eventually she got up and hugged her mother's knees, sobbing loudly. Sharon picked her up and they cuddled.

A discipline technique carried out by a number of mothers in response to a situation in which their child hurts another child, was to pay a lot of attention to the child who was hurt and ignore their own child who had inflicted the hurt. This was the way in which the playgroup leader of the suburban group advised mothers to deal with these situations. The effect of this disciplinary action was the same as described above. The child experienced the withdrawal of the mother and then they both experienced a desire to make up with each other.

The suburban and alternative mothers overwhelmingly confirmed the emotional experience involved in the reparative discipline cycle during their interviews. When I talked to the suburban and alternative mothers about getting angry with their children, they mentioned feeling 'terrible' or 'guilty' afterwards and some mentioned feeling sorry themselves for getting so angry. The following replies from the suburban mothers are illustrative:

> Sarah usually makes me feel guilty; she'll come up and say, 'Sorry mummy', you know and then we'll both have a little cry or a cuddle or something and we make friends.

> breaks her heart if I yell at her, or something . . . [and then I feel] terrible . . . I wait until she comes to me. Sometimes I, like, if she's starting to throw tantrums I just pick her up and put her in her room and I say, don't come out until you stop it, and she comes out, and there's tears, and 'Oh, mummy, mummy', so I pick her up.

> Usually Kylie comes out and says 'I'm sorry mummy . . . I love you'. I'm so annoyed she can do that! . . . Because you're trying to teach them and they, 'Oh, but I love you'. And you think, Oh well, how can I be angry with this child?

> After I've had a bad day, you know, I go to bed and I can't sleep for worrying about having punished her. And I feel like I'm too harsh on her sometimes.

I suggest that the mother's orientation towards healing the relationship becomes patterned by the singular care-giving relationship, in which the mother feels personally responsible for her child's comfort needs. The mother's feeling of responsibility for the child's comfort needs comes into a tension with the mother's feeling of responsibility for the child's social behaviour and patterns this cyclical effect.

However, the cyclical effect of the disciplinary action taken by the suburban mothers was noticeably lacking in the disciplinary action taken by a number of the kinship mothers. The child's experience of distress at the mother's expressions of anger was not so apparent in this group.

Thus, as we shall now see, the predominant maternal attitude shapes the outcome of maternal-infant conflict.

The kinship group

Disciplinary action was more linear than cyclical in the kinship group. Relations vacillated back and forth from mother dominance to child dominance. As I have already pointed out, there was very little involvement by mothers in the kinship playgroup in the activities of their children. Mothers sat inside for the most part while their children played outside. The children came in to be comforted by their mothers, or their carer for the morning, if they were hurt by one of the other children, but mothers did not follow them outside to protect them, or supervise their play. Their attitude towards caring for their children was more strategic than orientated towards understanding.

The kinship mothers did not generally anticipate situations that might lead to conflict, and did not supervise, or protect their children in the play area. As a result, one child became the dominant child in the play area and constantly performed aggressive acts on the other children and his mother had to keep up a barrage of admonishments to her child. However, her son, Tim, showed no emotional reaction to his mother's threats and expressions of anger whatsoever, although he screamed in rage when his mother took a toy away from him and gave it back to a little girl.

In order to elicit some emotional reaction from her child, apart from rage, Tim's mother eventually indulged in extreme, physical forms of punishment. For example, towards the end of playgroup one morning, Tim bit another little boy who screamed out in pain. His mother, who by this stage was very frustrated, went out and bit her son extremely hard. Tim also screamed out in pain. After a short time, he came inside and climbed up on his mother's knee, sobbing loudly. He put his bitten arm up to his mother's face for her to kiss better.

While comforting her son, the mother told me that 'you have to bite him harder than he has bitten the other child, otherwise it has no effect'. It certainly did have an immediate effect. However, it was an effect induced by the experience of physical pain, rather than the withdrawal of his mother's love. Tim wanted comfort, but he did not appear to show any signs of remorse. As soon as he felt comforted, he hopped down from his mother's knee and went back outside to play. The first thing that he did was to lift up the trampoline that two little girls were playing on and they almost fell onto the ground.

Tim's case was certainly one of the more extreme examples of antisocial behaviour that I observed. Other social relations in the kinship group were by no means as extreme. However, only two of the kinship mothers described experiencing a period of reconciliation like that described by the vast majority of suburban and alternative mothers. Most of the kinship mothers also talked to me about how difficult it was for them to get their children to do what they were told at home, and they tended to describe much more physically extreme methods of disciplining their children and expected other parents to apply harsh, physical punishment if their children 'deserved it'.

As an extreme case, Tim's example serves to illustrate disciplinary action that relies almost exclusively on subject-object relations. Because there is no-one attempting to understand him, or anticipate his actions and possible sources of conflict, interaction with his mother is limited almost entirely to trying to direct his behaviour after he has indulged in anti-social acts.

The alternative group

The reparative discipline pattern also occurred in the alternative dyads. Although anti-social acts had little opportunity to eventuate, when they did and they were seen by the mother, she would quickly respond in a similar way to the suburban mothers. For example, one morning Liem, who was 18 months old, began to hit another little boy over the head with the branch of a tree. His mother, Josie, immediately went over and told him that he had hurt the little boy. She then ignored Liem and took the little boy by the hand, leading him back to his aunt who was minding him. His aunt cuddled and kissed the little boy who had been hurt on the forehead and the little boy wept loudly. Meanwhile, Liem walked back up the hill and sat on his mother's knee. He took out her breast and began to suck. Josie assisted him and cuddled him while he sucked.

However, the alternative mothers tended to experience aspects of the cycle even more intensely than the suburban mothers. Like a few of the more child-centred suburban mothers, the alternative mothers believed that anger was an ugly emotion, having no positive value in their relationship with their children. When I asked alternative mothers about getting angry with their children, they were, in the main, reluctant to admit that they did get angry with their children and always qualified their statements to me about this with a justification, such as Karen's, 'I was feeling really, just like, exhausted . . . I'd reached my limit'.

The desire of these mothers to make amends with their children was acutely felt:

> [After I've yelled at him, I feel] terrible. I've thought, 'oh, that was a bit heavy handed. You don't need to do that to get the message to him.' Then I'd probably apologise to him, sort of comfort him. And more recently I'd say, 'look, I'm sorry, you know, I didn't mean to make you that upset, but you know, I'm really tired' or, you know, 'I wish you just wouldn't do that', try and explain it . . .

> [After I've gotten angry with him I feel] terrible, of course. Usually it goes over pretty quick, that horrible feeling, and I usually apologise to him, and say, 'Look, I'm sorry I got angry, I was just a bit tired and couldn't handle it.'

Like the more child-centred mothers in the suburban group, the alternative mothers found the tension between always wanting to gratify their child and the need to impose some limits on their child very stressful. However, if they were able to withdraw from their child, and allow their child to experience this loss, the children behaved very much like the children in the suburban group. They became distressed and showed signs of wanting to make up with their mother.

The reparative discipline cycle and surrogate-care providers

The adult involved in a reparative discipline cycle need not be the mother, or indeed any biological relation to the child, but the adult must be attached to the child. Trudy, for example, had minded her friend's 15 month-old child, Michael, every weekday since Michael was 6 weeks old. She told me that she was very attached to him and Michael appeared to be attached to her.

One morning, Michael was playing in the toilet. Trudy decided that she ought to stop him from playing there and went over and removed him bodily, placing him down outside in the yard. Michael looked at Trudy and motioned his intention to go straight back into the toilet. Trudy said 'No', loudly and firmly. Michael cried and motioned his intention to go to the toilet once again. Trudy continued to say 'No'. Michael sank to the ground sobbing loudly. Eventually he quietened down a little and went over and hugged Trudy around the knees. She picked him up and gave him a cuddle.

Trudy's relationship with her friend's infant is unusual, however, by alternative care provider standards. Trudy believed in treating Michael just as she would her own child, even though this meant that she became very attached to Michael and found it very difficult to give him back to his parents at night. According to Trudy, Michael also found it difficult to return to his parents' home at night, crying and clinging to her on separation. Trudy found this situation very painful.

The difficulty that alternative care providers find in following the 'mothering model' when caring for other children has been investigated by Margaret Nelson (1990). After analysing the results of a survey of 225 family day-care providers, she concluded that these carers 'held back' in their relations with the children, following a 'detached attachment' model so as to avoid the problem experienced by Trudy. Alternative carers usually recognize that it is the parents who ultimately have the direct responsibility for their children's social behaviour. They recognize the limits to their authority and may feel powerless to intervene on behalf of the child. Alternative care providers may deliberately remain more aloof from children in their care.

According to Nelson (1990: 599), it is also much easier for an alternative care provider to get children to comply with their demands. Alternative carers do not usually become involved in 'the life-or-death power struggle' which mothering entails. Apart from Trudy, alternative carers in the sample were only 'part-time' carers. Although they were usually affectionate towards the children and were sought out by the children if they needed comfort, I did not observe alternative care providers getting angry with the children in their care at playgroup. Children in this situation usually responded to firm commands.

When other adults chastise a child the reparative cycle is not brought into effect. As I mentioned previously, it rarely happens that a mother chastises another mother's child except if the mother is out of sight. I did observe two occasions when this happened and in both instances the child immediately complied with the adult's order. However, they also became very distressed and required comforting by the mother.

I spoke to a number of mothers in playgroup about the compliance of young children when spoken to by an unattached adult, and there was general agreement that children are 'always better behaved for someone else'. This also appeared to be the case on those occasions when I was asked to supervise children so that the mothers could have a meeting. Children whom I had observed often refusing to do what their mothers wanted them to do were very obedient when their mothers were out of sight and I asked them to do something. Thus, the presence of the mother, or an attached adult, would appear to give the child a feeling of power. The child's experience of this power is necessary to bring the reparative cycle into effect.

Fathers and the reparative discipline cycle

Some of the fathers who were more involved in the care of their children also experienced this cycle, although they did not appear to go through it with quite the same intensity. Ross, for example, was one of the 'role swap' fathers, who said simply: '. . . and then they start crying and I feel sorry, and it's all over type of thing'.

Paul cared for his children when his wife worked part time. Unlike the majority of mothers in my sample, his wife referred to him as 'the soft one'. He didn't feel 'the greatest' after he had smacked his daughter and usually ended up 'giving her a cuddle' when his daughter wanted to make up, at which point he would talk to her about why she had got a smack.

Christine's husband, Mark, also spent considerable time caring for his young child while his wife worked part time. However, Christine's intense feelings of guilt after an angry outburst with her child were not matched in degree by Mark's comments. Mark said simply that he felt 'better sometimes, worse sometimes' after giving his child a smack.

Neither were John's comments matched in intensity with some of the mother's comments. John was a 'role swap' father who cared for his daughter, Jodie, from 12 months of age. John 'didn't enjoy' smacking his daughter but felt that it was sometimes necessary. If his wife was also home, his daughter went to the mother for consolation, rather than her father. If they were home on their own, Jodie went to her room and came out when she was over it. They did not have an intense reunion. Instead, John would 'try and act as if things were normal again' and he would explain to her again why she had got smacked.

All of the suburban and alternative mothers in my sample were affected by their children's distress and experienced a desire to make up with their children after they punished them. However, in the very small sample of fathers that I interviewed, neither of the two fathers who worked long hours away from their children experienced feelings of remorse. Barry, for example, told me:

> . . . as I've said, my wife's a lot softer than I. For instance, if they muck up around tea time as far as I'm concerned they can go to bed without their tea and come out at breakfast time. But that's not Mary's ideas, you know, she tries to get round it in a different way.

Although it appears that involved fathers are more likely to experience remorse following conflict with their children than non-involved fathers, none of the fathers that I interviewed appeared to want to do anything special for their child afterwards, to make up. Compare the involved fathers with, for example, the mother who went and got the child's bottle as a treat. Even involved fathers, at least in my sample, did not appear to be as involved with their children as the mother. And unlike many of the mothers, no father seemed to feel any need to justify their actions to the child, in terms of their angry outburst being, in part, their own failing. They all felt that their actions were justified.

Diffuse care-giving and disciplinary action
When there are a number of carers involved in the day-to-day care and discipline of young children, it can be difficult for any one of them in particular to actualize the reparative discipline cycle, unless the question of who is directly responsible for defining child-rearing situations has been clearly worked out. The single mothers who lived with their own mothers came up against this problem.

As I have already mentioned, many of these mothers lived with their own mothers who found it difficult not to intervene in their daughter's definitions of the child's needs. As a consequence, they inadvertently undermined their daughter's attempts to discipline their children. Sandra, for example, told me how her mother was always around the corner, ready to give her child a biscuit when she was trying to punish her. This prevented the child from experiencing the mother's 'loss', since she always had another 'mother' to indulge her. If the child does not experience the loss of the mother's love, there is no opportunity for the child to experience the desire to heal their relationship with their mother.

Diffuse care-giving appears as a structural variable in the emergence of different forms of subjectivity. Unless the adults involved make a conscious decision about the question of personal responsibility, a singular care-giving relationship will not eventuate. In the suburban and alternative groups, parents experienced a social boundary around their domestic unit, within which they experienced direct, personal responsibility both for the well-being of their child and their child's social behaviour. Other living arrangements may also provide opportunities for the child to experience a reparative discipline cycle, but the question of personal responsibility needs to be clarified by the adults concerned.

Case studies of 'misunderstanding'

There were individual cases in the suburban group of mothers who did not appear to be able to differentiate their own perspective from that of the child, and assert a clear dividing line between two sets of interests. Their perspective and the perspective they held of their child seemed to be almost totally fused, even though these mothers made great efforts to try to understand their child's point of view. As a result, the children did not experience their mothers as separate selves, but as part of their own self and like some of the kinship children, failed to show any remorse when they were punished by the mother. I have prepared the following case studies to illustrate this problem of misunderstanding.

Julie

Julie is a suburban mother with one son, Jason, aged 3 years. She is married to the father of the child and living in a nuclear family arrangement. She has worked part time doing general secretarial work since having Jason and while she is working her mother minds her son. Julie has also completed a two-year training course in animal nursery at the technical college and she is keen to get some work eventually in this field. Her husband is a shift worker doing 'mundane, production line stuff'. They were both on unemployment benefits for some time before having Jason and the husband is still in and out of work.

Julie attends playgroup irregularly because of her work commitments. Sometimes she brings Max, the 3 year-old son of her friend, whom she minds while her friend is at work. She comes to playgroup because there are no other children in her neighbourhood and she is very worried that Jason will not be able to handle preschool when he begins next year. She told me how 'overprotective' her own mother was and she does not want to be the same with Jason.

Jason is a very big boy for his age. When I first saw them, Jason was sitting on his mother's knee, alternating between hugging her tightly and punching her hard. I sat down next to her and she immediately began to tell me how embarrassing it was for her that all the other children seemed to be playing but her son would not leave her. She had an explanation for her son's behaviour which directly reflected her own memories of being 'terrified' at social gatherings. Mixed in with comments about her own childhood, were critical comments about the way her mother treated Jason. She believed that her mother was undermining her own attempts to bring Jason up without suffering the same problems she had suffered.

While we were talking on the first morning, Jason got down from his mother's knee and went over to the climbing frame. He began to climb up the net but only got half way before Julie yelled out urgently 'Be careful!' Jason immediately climbed down and came back and sat on her knee. I told him what a good climber I thought he was and Jason went off again to climb. This time he got to the top before Julie called out to him not to climb over the top onto the platform. (I had seen many younger children do this quite safely.) Jason came straight back down and climbed back on his mother's knee. I told him again that I thought it was a good climb. This time Julie also tried to be encouraging. 'Yes', she said 'it was a good climb', and Jason went off again.

That first morning I did not see Julie attempt to get either of the boys involved in any activity. Max just stood and watched all the other children play and shook his head when I offered him fruit at morning tea. I did see Julie at the climbing frame later in the morning, holding on tightly to Jason's hand. I noticed that Jason was caressing his mother, very intensely.

This pattern was repeated the next time I saw Julie at playgroup. When she arrived she sat down with Jason on her knee, clasping him tightly. When I sat next to her, she recounted how embarrassing Jason's behaviour was for her. 'I wouldn't put myself through it if I didn't think it was what he needed', she complained, 'I'm sure there are plenty of other mothers with children like this but they just don't go out. Mum doesn't help, she's so critical of everything that I do, but I need her to look after him while I work.'

On this occasion, I noticed that Jason got down from his mother's knee and tugged at his mother's hand, wanting her to follow. Her response, however, was to cling more tightly to him, then push him away from her. I suggested that we both follow Jason and see what he wanted, but Julie said that it was alright and that he would eventually settle down. After continued and more intense tugging I stood up and suggested again that we follow. Julie stood up and we both followed Jason who immediately began to wander around the play area. While we were following, Julie complained bitterly about her own mother. 'She never had any time for me when I was a child; she was always cleaning . . .'

The next time I saw Julie at playgroup, I was surprised to see her standing over by the climbing frame, watching and encouraging Jason and Max on the play activities. When I walked over, I noticed that the boys were really enjoying themselves this morning. I stopped to chat and told Julie how nice for her to have the boys so well settled into playgroup and Julie was obviously pleased.

However, while I was talking to Julie I noticed how much Jason was commanding his mother's attention. He directed all his efforts at his mother and expected her to watch continually and applaud him. When he ran down the hill, he ran into his mother; when he climbed up the net he used her as a ladder. It was as if his mother was his own, personal object. He touched her often, squeezing her hard and he often fondled her breasts. If she was not paying attention he would punch her or bite her. Once, I saw him bite her on the breast.

During my interview with Julie, it was most apparent that Julie was an extremely anxious mother, who tried desperately to figure out what was wrong with her child. Her account of the first few weeks is full of her explanations of why her child was crying: 'I found that Jason was really sensitive to a lot of noise and my room [in the hospital] was right next to the nurse's station'; 'his bed had this horrible, stiff lining underneath, he was just laying on a piece of hard, flat, kapok or whatever they use to put on the bottom of the crib. He had one blanket on him . . . the poor kid was probably cold and he was getting woken up through the night all the time.'

Julie believed that as the child's mother everyone would expect her to know what he needed and be able to satisfy him. She was in constant fear of Jason being out of her control; of Jason 'not doing anything I wanted him to do'. Although she was able to get the care of Jason 'down pat' at home, it was not so easy for her when in social situations, as the following extract of her outing with Jason to a Tupperware party when he was 6 weeks old demonstrates:

Ten minutes after I got there he started to get upset, so I fed him. He was still upset. By the time we got to the stage of going home, he was screaming. I mean it was so noisy and I took him out to the kitchen. I couldn't console him. He'd had a needle the day before and I was starting to think that was affecting him. And the people were coming and saying 'What's wrong with your baby, love?' and I said 'look, I don't know' and I was getting real upset.

As soon as Julie put Jason in the car to take him home he fell asleep. Her final explanation for his crying was:

he just didn't want to be around all these people. As young as he was, he knew. And to this day he'll do the same thing. Even when I bring him here [to playgroup] sometimes he won't want to come in. And he's always been like that. He just doesn't like crowds of people . . . you take him to birthday parties, like in a room full of kids, you wouldn't be able to get him in the door. You'd have to scrape him off the wall to get him in the door . . . and he wouldn't stay there. You'd have to close the door so he wouldn't get out, and then he'd be standing there banging on the door trying to get out. There's an open window, he'd be out of that.

Although Julie was full of criticism about the way she was brought up and about the way her mother undermines her authority, her mother is the only person she will consider leaving Jason with when she works. She believes Jason is 'a little bit of an escape artist' and her mother is the only person she can trust to watch over him constantly.

> I can go somewhere if I leave him with mum. Mum hovers over him. She doesn't let him out of her sight. Even if he's out in the yard she's got to go out with him. I know that nothing would ever happen to him while she's with him.

She is happy to have her husband, Paul, look after Jason if she is called in to work and her mother's out shopping. Even though 'he's not as vigilant as what she [her mother] is' Julie can always trust him to know what Jason is doing and in any case 'Jason usually stays closer to him when I'm not there.'

Trying to discipline Jason involved Julie in extreme acts of physical violence, as the following episode she recounted to me illustrates:

> I was getting out of the shower and had no clothes on. Jason came up behind me and bit me on the backside, and it hurt, you know? And I just swung around, just pushed him like that, and he sort of walked six steps backwards, fell into the hallway, and I picked him up and whacked him about six times across the back of the leg. I said 'I've told you never to do that.' And he really got upset to the stage where he was sick. And then I felt terrible. But I mean I still wore the scar. I mean it drew blood and everything.

Julie then recounted how they cuddled and made up and she told me that he had stopped biting her now. (However, I had seen him bite her in playgroup.) Julie says that she must use harsh physical violence because its the only way she can control Jason:

> Once, when I was in the laundry, Jason turned the gas oven on. He'd turned it on full, and it stunk and we've got birds in the house. He could have gassed us all. I roused [scolded] on him for doing that, but because I didn't know how long ago he'd done it I didn't smack him. Two nights later I'm out doing the potatoes and he came up behind me and he turned it on again and I said 'don't' and shouted at him and I said 'don't you ever do that again', and he laughed at me. And I said 'you'll get the fly swatter'. And I turned around like that and he put his hand out to do it again. So the fly swatter it was. Not hard, but it stung. He just stood there and he just walked away and I felt awful . . . It didn't leave a mark, but it just stung, just a little bit, and I thought 'oh'. But he didn't do it again.

I have used Julie's case study to demonstrate what misunderstanding the perspective of the child would mean. Although the outcome of

Julie's efforts to discipline her son is similar to those I observed in the kinship group, Julie's case differs in that she makes desperate attempts to understand her child. She is constantly constructing an elaborate perspective for her child and she experiences the personal responsibility for Jason's welfare acutely.

However, in constructing this perspective, Julie relies almost totally on her own perspective as an adult, recalling how she felt as a child. She feels so 'fused' with her child that she appears to be unable to see that two perspectives exist and as a result does not attempt 'to read the cues' of her child as a separate being. Her arrival behaviour at playgroup is an apt illustration of this. She clasps him to her and believes he is as anxious of the social situation as she is, even though he quite obviously wants to explore, so long as his mother accompanies him. Instead of trying to understand what Jason is attempting to communicate to her, Julie's interpretation of this situation draws entirely on her own experience. She then attempts to impose this interpretation of the situation onto Jason.

Jason's behaviour also demonstrates this 'fusion' of perspectives. He treats his mother like an object, caressing and fondling her body whenever he likes. He would use her body as an object whenever he felt the need. His constant demand for her applause reflects the lack of self-satisfaction he is able to achieve. He only finds it worthwhile, or satisfying, to do something if he receives his mother's recognition for it. I did not observe him participating in any activity that was satisfying for him in itself.

Only extreme physical acts appeared to demarcate the separate existence of the mother and child. Julie does not notice Jason's more subtle cues, so that Jason must punch and bite his mother in order to get her to notice his separateness. Julie experiences this action as resistance to her control, requiring extreme counter-measures.

Michelle

Michelle is a suburban mother with one child, Claire, aged $2^1/2$ years. She is 20 weeks pregnant with her second child. She is married to the father of the child and living in a nuclear family arrangement. Before having Claire, Michelle was a receptionist and has worked part time as a receptionist since Claire was very young. While she works, her mother-in-law looks after Claire and she is very happy about this arrangement because her in-laws 'idealize Claire'.

When I first observed Michelle with her daughter I thought that she was a 'prompt and avid follower'. She followed her daughter from one activity to another and I noticed how concerned she was to make the most of every opportunity to teach her child to share and be considerate of others. However, after a while of observing her, I began to think that her intervention was so constant as to be intrusive. Claire was never left to play by herself.

For example, one morning I was watching Claire playing in the sand-pit. She was pouring sand down a funnel into a bucket. Michelle intervened and made her hold the funnel a little lower in case the sand blew into the smaller children's eyes. A short time later, Claire took a spade from another little girl. Michelle took the spade away from Claire and gave it back to the little girl, explaining to Claire that there were many other spades around the sandpit that she could use. This type of intervention was constant throughout the morning. Michelle seemed very anxious to make sure Claire was always behaving correctly.

The next time I saw Michelle at playgroup, I was again struck by her constant intervention, which always contained a rationale that Michelle was trying to teach her. It was 'Give that one back, Claire', 'there's another over here, Claire', 'you might hurt Eliza if you do that like that, Claire'. As the morning wore on, I began to notice that Claire was getting more and more irritated with her mother's constant intervention. Eventually, she got so cross with her mother that she hit her. Michelle grabbed Claire's arm and smacked her very lightly on the bottom and Claire threw herself to the ground, screaming. Michelle went back to her seat. Claire eventually calmed down and continued playing as she had done before her mother's interruption.

Claire did not appear to show any effect from the smack, other than rage at her mother, which finally abated. However, her behaviour became more and more anti-social over the duration of my stay with this group. She would take things from children and hit them and throw sand over the other children. Michelle's attempts at intervention appeared to have little effect, other than provoking more anti-social behaviour.

During my interview with Michelle I was struck by her inability to assert her own interests over Claire's. For example, she had only wanted to breast-feed Claire for about nine months, but was still 'waiting for her to give it up' at two and a half years. She could not confront any conflict of interest with Claire and as soon as she anticipated a conflict, she immediately tried to soothe things over, before any confrontation could take place.

When I asked her how she went about constraining Claire, or setting limits, she replied that if Claire is doing something she does not want her to do, she will try to distract her. If this does not work, and reasoning fails, then she will attempt to smother her and Claire's angry feelings in cuddles:

> I can just sit her down and give her a cuddle and get sooky rather than angry with her and smack her. I just say 'come on, be mummy's baby', and we'll have a big cuddle and a sing song or something. That'll usually calm her down. And maybe then I can coax her into coming and lying down.

I persisted for some time with this line of questioning, trying to get Michelle to talk about *her* angry feelings, rather than her child's:

Q. But do you ever have to get angry with her?

A. Oh, yes, when I'm just not in the mood, you know. There were times when, especially in the early stages of this pregnancy when I was a bit, I wasn't that sick, but I was worn out all the time, and there were times when I felt as though I was neglecting her really. I just felt like I couldn't be bothered doing anything. I just wanted to sit there and I'd wish she'd just go away and amuse herself.

Q. But did you get angry?

A. Yeah, oh yeah. But I mean, sometimes I get angry. I'll give her a smack and afterwards I think that she didn't really need to have a smack then. I could've got out of it in other ways.

Q. And how does that make you feel?

A. I feel guilty.

Q. What do you do then?

A. She's not a crying child. Doesn't cry a lot unless she's really upset. Usually she's just shocked that she's been smacked, because she's probably not expecting it, or she doesn't think she's deserved it . . . Eventually I calm myself down, take a big breath and think, 'this isn't being fair to her' or other times I'll think 'no, she did deserve it' and I'll say 'go to your room' or 'go away. I don't want to see you if you're going to be naughty. I only want to see a happy girl'.

Michelle was extremely reluctant to even admit that she did get angry, and when she finally did she was very concerned to explain her anger as her own failing. She immediately tried to suppress her angry feelings when they appeared, so that Claire never had to experience the withdrawal of her mother. However, it seemed from my observations of their interaction and Michelle's comments that Claire was not at all reluctant to express her anger! But it was Michelle who felt 'guilty' and sought forgiveness from Claire. Claire did not have to seek forgiveness from her mother.

Catherine

Catherine is a suburban mother with one child, Nick, aged 3 years. She was over 30 when she had Nick and is now at home full time. Her husband works in a managerial position. She comes to playgroup with a friend and they sit together for most of the morning, rarely mixing with the other mothers.

Nick engages in a great deal of anti-social behaviour. If another child picks up a toy, or gets a bike out to ride, Nick will often take it away from the other child. I often observed him throwing sand and hitting other children in situations that appeared to be unprovoked.

Nick's mother rarely gets involved in his play. She sits and chats with her friend. Sometimes she will look up when she hears a child cry out, as a result of Nick's actions, and then she will call out to her son to 'stop that'. Whenever she chastises him more firmly, it does not appear to have any effect on him whatsoever, except that if she keeps it up he is likely to get very irritated with his mother and go into a rage. He got so angry with his mother one morning for asking him to stop piling sand up on the climbing frame that he threw the sand at her. She did not get angry with him for this, but simply walked away.

I never saw Catherine get angry with Nick, even though she witnessed a number of incidents in which he hurt another child. Instead, she would reason with him and explain to him why he should not do that. Nick never showed any sign that he was listening and did not obey his mother's commands.

She would, though, give an explanation for his behaviour to anyone who was prepared to listen. For example, one morning I watched him try to take a bucket away from a girl in the sandpit. The little girl hung on to the bucket and Nick hit her over the head with a spade. She let it go and ran inside crying to find her mother. Catherine was sitting beside the sandpit and watched the whole incident. She did not chastise Nick but explained to me that this was a fight between Nick and the little girl that had been going on for some weeks. According to Catherine, the little girl had tipped a bucket of sand over Nick's head some weeks ago. She excused Nick's behaviour with 'Nick never forgets. He is more like an adult than a child.'

Her friend supported her with the comment that 'children should learn to stand up for themselves, don't you think?' Catherine then told me about Nick's 'strong personality'. She said it was difficult for her to discipline him away from home, because the only technique she used for controlling him was to send him to his room.

I was struck by Catherine's calmness in the face of Nick's ongoing anti-social behaviour. She appeared just to accept his behaviour as being part of his personality which she interpreted as 'strong'. The other mothers at playgroup thought of Nick as a bully. There was an element of ambiguity in Catherine's rationale, however, in that she conceded some aspects of his behaviour were undesirable. However, she felt there was nothing she could do to modify these aspects. She regarded him as an adult who could only be won over by persuasion.

Catherine expected Nick to understand from an adult's point of view. She did not appear to understand that a child's perspective requires a different standpoint. Unlike mothers who take the attitude of the child by moving backwards and forwards from the child to the adult perspective, Catherine had only one vantage point and expected Nick to understand this as an adult might, by being reasonable.

When Catherine chastised Nick at playgroup, the results were similar to those I have described above as embedded in subject-object relations. Nick showed very little emotional reaction to his mother's admonishments and if they continued, he flew into a rage which he directed at his mother.

The role of the body and its connection to the 'social'

The cases of misunderstanding that I have described serve to illustrate that understanding a child involves certain psychological capacities, as well as linguistic competence. Understanding has an hermeneutic dimension, but this dimension cannot be separated from the psychological make-up of the mother. Misunderstanding did not simply occur because the mother misread the cues of her child. It occurred because of emotional difficulties in the mother that were aggravated by social conditions which intensified the mother's feeling of personal responsibility for the welfare and social behaviour of her child. In Julie's case, these difficulties related to her own feelings of social insecurity. Michelle found the experience of emotional withdrawal from her child too painful for her to assert herself over the child. Catherine did not express any feelings of anger to her child.

Psychoanalysts may well be able to explain the particular attitudes that these mothers adopted towards their children in terms of individual psychopathologies. It is not my intention to uncover the idiosyncratic psychopathologies that may or may not exist in these mothers, nor the potential neurosis that may or may not develop in the children. What is important for the reader to grasp is the interrelationship of the cognitive and affective dimensions of maternal attitudes. Maternal attitudes cannot be reduced to their cognitive component, that is, child-rearing ideals and belief systems although these play an important role. There are also crucial psychological competences underlying maternal attitudes that are connected to the broader social context in which women mother.

Central to the psychological competence required to bring the reparative discipline cycle into effect is the strength of the maternal Ego, that is the mother's self-confidence and self-assertiveness. I suggest that this competence is directly connected to the status of women in any particular society and any individual mother's own potential to achieve autonomy.

Critical theorists have attempted to analyse the way in which an autonomous self is constructed: a 'coherent' self, 'capable of utilizing culture while at the same time maintaining a critical distance from it' (Alford 1987: 25). I have attempted to demonstrate that it is not sufficient simply to conceive of the autonomous subject as an individual who is self-assertive and able to take a critical stance. It is also necessary to analyse how the autonomous subject develops moral attitudes that can accommodate another's claim to autonomy. In my view, an emancipatory morality involves the construction of individual subjectivities that are capable of experiencing concern for those who are less powerful. The purpose of my study has been to illuminate the relational nature of the construction of such emancipated subjectivities.[3]

When we consider that one self is constructed in relation to another self, it is no longer possible to assume that the autonomous subject idealized by critical theory will simply emerge developmentally. This subject must be actively produced and in our society the actors involved continue to be overwhelmingly women. Contemporary feminists have shown convincingly that this responsibility places the mother in a different relation to the economy and the state than the father, and that this relation undermines the mother's own achievement of personal autonomy as defined by the enlightenment tradition. What, then, are the political implications of the study? In the concluding chapter, I discuss these, using Habermas' thesis of the colonization of the lifeworld as a model.

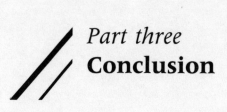

Part three
Conclusion

8 // The politics of the particular and the generalized 'other'

Autonomy as a relational concept

As Carole Pateman (1989: 118) has observed, feminism and liberalism have a common origin 'in the emergence of individualism as a general theory of social life'. Common to both doctrines is the goal of individual emancipation, of breaking away from the confines of ascriptive ties, derived from traditional ways of life. This is an objective known as the project of modernity. Feminism has its own roots firmly located within this project.

The problem for women, however, is that the project of modernity is closely tied to the liberal philosophical tradition which three decades of feminist scholarship has shown to be oppressive to women. Liberalism is inherently oppressive to women because its foundations are grounded in a division of social life into separate public and private spheres. It is the public sphere that is individuated, through the subject's legal status as a citizen and as a worker. However, the reproduction of future citizens and workers is performed largely by women in the private sphere, which remains particularized and non-individuated. Thus, liberalism emancipates men at the expense of confining women.

Feminist analyses of liberalism tend, therefore, to regard the construction of these two spheres of social life as separate and distinct as inherently patriarchal.[1] The argument is that although women may gain the same formal rights as men, their responsibility for child-rearing activity continues to disadvantage them in the public sphere of life. The extension of universal rights to women will not overcome the different relation in which men and women stand to work and public life so long as women continue to bear the primary burden for child-rearing.[2]

Feminism's own grounding in the project of modernity presents contemporary feminists with a dilemma. How can the emancipatory potential of liberalism be extended to women, when emancipation, as defined by this tradition, depends upon privatizing and essentializing their experience as women?

I have confronted this dilemma by proposing an alternative conception of emancipation, which includes women's sphere of activity. Within the parameters of this alternative, individual autonomy appears as a form of subjectivity that must be actively produced by another whose own claim to autonomy must also be successfully asserted. There are crucial differences here with critical theory's notion of an emancipated subjectivity. These differences have important consequences for considering the political implications of the study.

Critical theory's autonomous subject

Critical theory's conception of autonomy still has strong links to Weber's (1958) rational individual, who emerges in Weber's theory as the result of the rationalization of the Calvinist religious worldview. The link between Weber's and critical theory's autonomous subject is to be found in the idea that the autonomous subject is an isolated individual whose authenticity as a subject is constituted through the adoption of a rationally deduced value system.

Weber did not specify a psychological mechanism to explain why the individual subject would act towards others according to his or her rationally thought out value system. He did not need a psychological theory of internalization because he claimed that believers came under a religious compulsion to follow the tenets of Calvinism and control their personal conduct according to this value system.[3] Thus, the agent overseeing the production of Weber's subject was located in the other world, in God and religious doctrine. The fear of being one of God's damned provided the motive.

However, the Frankfurt philosophers, most notably Horkheimmer, did elaborate on the psychological mechanism necessary to constitute an autonomous individual. Their psychological model shifted the question of agency away from God and religious dogma to the patriarchal father. Using Freud's theory of internalization, the Frankfurt philosophers claimed that personal autonomy and personal authenticity became structured into the psyche by way of the internalization of paternal authority. They claimed that the internalization of paternal authority, within the structure provided by the patriarchal family, was necessary for the individual to develop a sufficiently strong ego to resist the social pressure to conform to mass society.[4]

The Frankfurt philosophers developed this theory to link the process of societal rationalization to the loss of individual autonomy. What they attempted to demonstrate was that the process of societal rationalization would ultimately destroy the autonomy and authenticity of individuals.

As the state expanded according to the logic of instrumental reason, it also took over the functions of the family and undermined paternal authority. They argued that as an outcome of this intrusion by the state into family life, a new personality type would develop. They referred to this new type of personality as 'narcissistic', a self-centred individual unable to take a moral stand against the pressures of mass opinion. Without the psychic benefits of the struggle with the father, they believed that the individual would not be able to offer any resistance to these impersonal, extra-familial forms of authority.

The thesis of the undermining of paternal authority has been reiterated in a number of forms since initially put forward by Horkheimmer in 1936.[5] Mitscherlich (1973) and Lasch (1977, 1978) have been particularly influential in their portrayal of contemporary society as fatherless and therefore 'narcissistic'. However, as Jessica Benjamin (1978: 51) has pointed out, the thesis of the fatherless society is forced to take a romanticized and nostalgic view of the patriarchal family of past times and to assume that human agency, in the form of an independent conscience, can only be achieved through the identification and struggle with an authoritarian father.

Moreover, the thesis of the fatherless society comes up against an impasse when it attempts to deal with women's claim to autonomy.[6] I suggest that this is because the mother's contribution to the creation of an autonomous subjectivity cannot be accommodated in a theory that takes the isolated individual actor as the phenomenon requiring explanation. With the isolated individual as the actor, it is impossible to locate the agency of the mother, structuring the child's claims to autonomy as she asserts her own. Critical theory has managed to avoid confronting this problem by relegating the mother's agency as nurturer to nature.

Habermas attempts to avoid Weber's impasse by switching to the philosophy of language, but in so doing loses sight of the fundamental psychological processes required to produce an authentic subjectivity altogether. Habermas does this by switching from a psychoanalytically informed model of socialization to a cognitive developmental learning model of socialization inspired by Jean Piaget and George Herbert Mead.

Habermas' learning model operates at two levels, at the collective or institutional level and at the level of individual socialization. At the collective level, norms that become rationalized through communicative action replace norms bound to tradition. These become institutionalized and are assimilated by children during the socialization process. Thus, children's personalities are becoming increasingly structured by social institutions that have been rationalized through communicative action. These norms are based on good reasons and remain open to critical reflection. Moreover, as children become communicatively competent, their own opportunities to assert their individual identities increase through the mechanism of communicative action.

However, the problem with Habermas' account of socialization is that it relies on G.H. Mead's developmental account of the constitution of the self. It lacks a relational account of the nurturing process and underplays the conflict of interests that are an inherent part of lifeworld interaction. Following Mead, Habermas sees competing claims to autonomy becoming structured in a 'complementary' fashion. This view of the socialization process masks the inherent conflict of interests that exist between actors, whose lifeworld interaction is guided by competing obligations and claims to autonomy, resolved in a field of unequal power relations.

While there has been sustained feminist criticism of the thesis of the fatherless society (Barrett and McIntosh: 1982), only the psychoanalytically inspired works of Jessica Benjamin and Nancy Chodorow have attempted to offer a feminist alternative to the grounding of moral authority in the patriarchal family. Both these writers elaborate a psychosocial account of the process of connectedness and individuation as the mechanism which constitutes the autonomy and authenticity of the individual. This alternative depends upon the assertion of the mother's subjectivity and has been most fully elaborated by Benjamin (1990) in her book, *The Bonds of Love*. I will consider Benjamin's alternative conception of autonomy in the light of the results of my study.

Jessica Benjamin's alternative: mutual recognition

Benjamin derives her basic concept of 'recognition' from Kohut's theory of the self, which she reworks as 'mutual recognition' in order to accommodate the mother as a subject in her own right. Although she draws on Habermas' notion of intersubjectivity in order to rework Kohut's concept of recognition as mutually constructed, she does not use the concept of intersubjectivity to depict an orientation towards understanding. Instead, she uses it to describe the necessity for both the mother and child to assert their own perspectives and recognize and confirm each other's separateness.

This is an important and central insight. However, it also has its limitations since the concept takes the need for mutual recognition for granted and thus cannot be used to explain how mutual recognition is brought about. I suggest that it would be more useful if the concept of intersubjectivity was reworked in a way that retained the interpretive dimension intended by Habermas' notion of communicative action.

Since Benjamin's concept of mutual recognition begins with the mother already 'knowing' her own child's 'needs', the interpretive dimension of nurturing activity is overlooked and the space in which nurturing is located can too easily be confined within a 'private' sphere. The public/private dichotomy is thereby reinforced, even if the lines are redrawn to allow for the extension of child-care facilities to assist parents with child-care tasks. Thus, even though Benjamin is committed to the feminist objective of making child-rearing a collective activity, she is caught with no social space but the 'private' to concretize nurturing activity.

Within Benjamin's scheme, nurturing cannot be concretized in the public sphere, or in civil society, through the action of abstracted individuals. It must therefore be concretized in the private sphere. Yet the nurturing process I call 'taking the attitude of the child' cannot be concretized within the confines of a domestic household. It is essentially a social process, involving the mother in a social sphere which extends beyond the bounds of the domestic household, out into a communally organized social space. While nurturing, carers find it necessary to develop mutually beneficial ties with others outside the immediate domestic household, not only for practical assistance, but also to provide common standards by which they can assess and evaluate their nurturing activity. Thus, nurturing activity requires a particularized action context that is also social, but this does not mean that this social space is 'private' in the sense that it lies outside public concern and collective obligation.

Benjamin's alternative to paternal authority depends upon the mother sustaining a balance between recognizing her child and asserting her own set of interests, but the concept of 'mutual recognition' is limited as an explanatory device. It cannot explain, for example, why the mother would retain this balance. Why would the mother not pursue her own autonomy and her own interests to the detriment of her child's need for 'recognition'?

The answer to this question lies in the normative context of nurturing activity. Mothers are under intense pressure to 'know' and be able to gratify their child's needs. The mother's motivation to care, to understand, or recognize a particular child, is constituted within this normative context. Once the mother has begun nurturing within this context, the actions of the child become a powerful motivating force. How, then, is this normative context open to change?

The normative context of nurturing activity is organized primarily through moral attitudes, rather than moral principles. Moral attitudes are not only structured through language, or competing principles, but also through the outcome of competing claims, or interests. Thus, child-centred maternal attitudes are subject to change as mothers question and critically reflect upon their ideals *and* as they assert their own claims to autonomy.

Mothers are increasingly recognizing their own rights and needs as individuals, but their assessment of their own interests is not always taken from the point of view of an isolated individual. Mothers weigh up and assess competing claims, including their own, according to their own value systems, sometimes as a member of a communally organized group and other times as individuals in their own right.

As Benjamin points out, the child needs to recognize the mother as a separate subject if the child is to acquire the capacity to acknowledge another's claim to autonomy. The assertion of the mother's set of interests is indeed an important aspect of this process and this has important political implications, but what, exactly, does the successful assertion of the mother's interests involve?

What this study demonstrates is that the mother's ability to assert herself against the demands of the child, and be recognized by her child as a separate subject, is only effective when the predominant relation between the mother and child has been patterned through understanding. Thus, there is nothing essential about the 'need' for mutual recognition. The assertion of the mother's subjectivity depends upon a number of contingent factors, including the predominant maternal attitude and associated child-rearing ideals, the status of women in a particular society and the meaning and value a particular culture, or subculture, attaches to the very notion of personal autonomy. While some of these contingent factors are the outcome of the mother's actions in concrete child-rearing situations, other factors, such as the status of women in a particular society and the mother's own opportunity for autonomy require action from a collective, political subject, committed to a feminist conception of emancipation. What contribution can this study make, then, to feminist politics?

Feminist politics and the rationalization of women's 'lifeworld'

Feminist political activists have attempted to re-cast the public/private divide in order to extend the emancipatory potential of liberalism to women. However, these attempts have been constrained by the very categories of 'public' and 'private'. Within the confines of these categories, the solution to women's subordination appears to lie in redrawing the lines which separate the categories, rather than reconceptualizing the categories themselves. Breaking down the liberal conception of public and private most often means extending the individuated logic of liberalism into what is still classically defined as a 'private' sphere.

Thus, although feminist analyses of the public/private distinction have successfully highlighted the way in which women have been disadvantaged in public life by their child-rearing responsibilities, there has been inadequate attention given to the re-conceptualization of the categories themselves. Social life still tends to be regarded as *either* public *or* private, yet neither of these categories can accommodate the social space in which child-rearing is actualized and the child's subjectivity 'produced'.

Rather than work with the public/private dichotomy, I have worked with the notions of individuated (or associative) and non-individuated (or communal) *action contexts*. The very notion of two action contexts draws attention to the fact that human agency exists at both levels, the generalizable and the particular. Thus, unlike Locke's conception of the private sphere, the communal action context in which nurturing activity is concretized, should not be considered as pre-determined by nature and therefore outside public concern or collective responsibility.

Another advantage of uncovering human agency at two levels of action, is that the limitations and possible 'pathologies' of political strategies which assume that there is only one level of human agency can be brought into focus. The question arises as to whether the extension of the individuating logic of liberalism into aspects of social life grounded in relations of personal interdependence, ultimately reifies the interpretive structures of social life and structures more oppressive human relationships. Can public policies for women's equality, that are enacted at the generalizable level, formalize the social relations of everyday life in such a way that women are prevented from negotiating the terms of their own particular situations, according to their own value systems?

This is the question underlying the thesis of 'the end of the individual', articulated in various forms by writers in the Weberian tradition. Habermas' thesis of the colonization of the lifeworld re-states this problematic. What is feared by writers in this tradition is that the extension of a universalizing and individuating logic into all aspects of everyday life will ultimately undermine our ability to order social life according to our own value systems. By bringing nurturing activity and the mothering culture into focus, it is possible to convey another pathological image of modernity, which deals with the construction of the self in relation to others.

This scenario could eventuate via the instrumentalization of nurturing practices, taking two possible routes. In the first instance, economic imperatives increasingly dominate maternal judgements. With individual family units having to accept the whole economic burden involved in caring for their dependent members and no alternative 'particular others' taking up the nurturing burden, mothers may increasingly have to become more pragmatic in their maternal judgements and be unable to accommodate either their own child-rearing ideals, or the agency of the child.

The second possibility would follow the path of bureaucratic, or administrative rationality. This would involve expert sub-cultures and state instrumentalities undermining the mothering culture. This possibility could eventuate either by the replacement of nurturing activity with state-administered child-rearing services, or by the confinement of nurturing activity within the domestic space of the private household. In this latter instance, mothers become more and more isolated from one another and are increasingly forced to rely upon expert subcultures for their maternal judgements. In either case, the mothering culture becomes a functional action context, in which children's needs become defined as a group, according to the imperatives of the economic and administrative systems (cf. Elshtain: 1983).[7]

With the undermining of the mothering culture, the agency of the child could no longer be accommodated in child-rearing practices and a different form of subjectivity would ensue. Even with the most utopian forms of democratization, the directly participatory agency of the mother and child in the constitution of cultural value systems and emancipatory forms of subjectivity would be lost to politicized forms of agency involving representation of pre-interpreted, collective interests. I suggest that in this modernity scenario, the potential for reparative forms of subjectivity would be undermined and replaced with more oppressive forms of subjectivity.

This image of modernity parallels Habermas' description of the colonization of the lifeworld. By clarifying two types of rationality, Habermas is able to depict both the positive and the negative outcomes of modernity. While his theory has a number of problems that need to be reworked from within a feminist perspective, his notion of the rationalization of the lifeworld can be usefully applied, with some modification, to women's struggles to rationalize the communal forms of social organization in which child-rearing is located. Feminist analyses of the family have been unable to locate women as critical agents within their families. I will discuss this idea, then return to the problem of colonization and feminist politics.

Communicative rationality and the family

According to feminist theory, the family is a central site of women's oppression. Habermas' claim is that social relations within families are subject to change through the medium of communicative action. We can imagine, for example, that under the impact of modernity, gendered roles open up to critical reflection. They are no longer determined by traditional modes of thought. Participants can decide to accept or reject the validity claims contained within them according to 'good reasons', which are context dependent. That is, their reasons for accepting or rejecting prescribed roles will depend upon their own particular situations.

This is the potentially liberating aspect of modernity. It is released into families through the mechanism of communicative action, through the potential for each adult family member to critically reflect upon gendered norms and interpret these according to the particularities of their own situation. This liberating potential flows through to socialization practices and restructures our social institutions. For example, Habermas (1987: 387) suggests that 'egalitarian patterns of relationship', 'individuated forms of intercourse' and 'liberalized child-rearing practices' reflect the realization of the potential of communicative action and the positive potential of societal rationalization to carry out the emancipatory project.

This liberating potential is also released into professional discourses, which have an inbuilt emancipatory dimension that is obscured in other sociological analyses of professional discourse. Pedagogy, for example, is based upon this orientation of trying to understand children and human relationships better. Thus, professional discourses are not only about the power-base of professional knowledge, nor only about normalizing deviants. These oppressive aspects of modernity show up in Habermas' theory via his thesis of the colonization of the lifeworld, when expert sub-systems lose their anchorage in the lifeworld.

Thus, in Habermas' view the contemporary family has not only been shaped by the functional needs of the economy and the state. The structural transformation of the bourgeois family also reflects the rationalization of the lifeworld. New family forms need to be seen as a product of the communicative rationality of members of the society. This means that there are positive, as well as negative outcomes, related to the communicative rationality that is then set free.

Habermas relies here on the 'differentiation' thesis. This is the thesis which holds that there is an increasing differentiation of society into more and more autonomous spheres of social life. The family is one such sphere. As it becomes differentiated out from other spheres, for example from the economy, it also becomes more autonomous with respect to these spheres. This changes the conditions for the socialization of individuals. There is greater potential for communicative action within families which counts towards the process of individuation for all.[8]

The family, then, cannot simply be analysed according to its contribution to the maintenance of the system. The family is 'deinstitutionalized' as are the communicative structures through which socialization takes place. Norms which are reproduced through socialization are increasingly becoming replaced by norms which are grounded in good reasons rather than traditional and religious modes of thought. Unlike the Frankfurt philosophers, who 'were forced to mourn the passing of the patriarchal family',[9] and those who now advocate, like Christopher Lasch, a return to some 'nostalgically loaded, frequently romanticized past of premodern forms of life' (Habermas 1987: 342), Habermas' way forward is not to retreat, but to build upon these mechanisms of communicative rationality that have been set free by modernity.

Whether or not the family can exist as an autonomous, self-contained and self-regulating unit is clearly crucial to Habermas' theory of emancipation. The crux of this theory is that participants must be free to agree to validity claims or not. Adults must have no other motive but the force of the better argument to consider when judging the validity of the norms which regulate their lives. The question is, how autonomous *is* the family and the members within it?

'The family' as an autonomous sub-system

Like Parsons, Habermas views the family as an autonomous sub-system, although unlike Parsons, he also sees the potential for action within the family to be communicatively rather than normatively regulated. However, Parsons' 'isolation' thesis has been challenged by numerous feminist scholars. Their critique focuses on two main areas. First, feminists have argued that the 'autonomous' family unit is itself a political and economic construct, a product of a particular political and economic system, which requires ongoing institutional support to sustain in this form. Within a feminist perspective of the family, the idea of an autonomous family unit is nonsensical without a corresponding conception of a collective body that is capable of sustaining and regulating it.

In other words, some form of state, or collective support and regulation is necessary to sustain the family in its apparently self-sufficient, 'isolated' form. Habermas sees state intervention only in terms of the constraints the state places on the autonomy of individuals within the family. He overlooks the fact that some form of collective *material* support is necessary if individuals within the family are to achieve 'autonomy'. Moreover, prior to the feminist engagement with the state, this public support appeared only to sustain the autonomy of men within the family, through helping to maintain their power over women.[10]

Second, the family still has very important links to kinship and communal forms of social organization and it continues to be largely women's work to maintain these links.[11] In Habermas' communicatively structured society, kinship and communal forms of social organization, in which women continue to live out the greater part of their everyday lives, seem either to be non-existent or else subject to the same form of rationalization, that is, through communicative action, as associative forms of social organization.

The problem here is that the fundamental organizing principle of communal forms of social organization are moral attitudes, rather than moral principles. Moral attitudes are structured by competing claims, or interests as well as the discursive content of norms. They are not directly amenable to change through communicative action. Habermas' 'free speech situation' can only be brought about for women involved in nurturing activity through some means of collective material support, to help equalize their claim to autonomy, since nurturing is located outside the current economic system.

Nancy Fraser's critique of Habermas' main concepts

My argument here has some parallels with Nancy Fraser's (1987) critique of Habermas' concept of communicative action. Fraser criticizes Habermas' inability to grasp the fact that men and women stand in a different relation to the state and the economy because of their child-rearing responsibilities. Habermas, she says, makes no allowance for the need for someone to be economically dependent while caring for children, yet his theory clearly depends upon someone performing this role. His distinction between symbolic and material reproduction (which corresponds to his distinction between communicative and strategic action) implies that child-rearing is located outside the dynamics of system reproduction. Yet this would make the person performing this task economically dependent (p. 43).

According to Fraser (pp. 49–50), the welfare state has structured a system in which the mother is defined as this dependent person. Men primarily claim benefits from the welfare state as an individual worker, or out-of-worker, while women tend to claim benefits primarily as dependent members of failed households. If her private means of support from a male breadwinner fail to eventuate, she becomes publicly dependent on the state.

Fraser rejects Habermas' distinctions, claiming that there is just as much symbolic reproduction (communicative action) involved in paid work as in child-rearing, and just as much instrumental/purposive activity involved in child-rearing as in other forms of work. She argues, in effect, that the lifeworld is already colonized, in that the media of money and power are already entrenched in the internal dynamics of the family. She sees no reason, then, for failing to extend the state into all child-rearing activity, since this, she believes, is the only way in which women will achieve the autonomy of men. Thus, she also rejects Habermas' distinction between what acts of the state constitute colonization and what acts constitute progress (p. 51).

Nancy Fraser's argument draws out the inability of Habermas' thesis to cope with the question of gender. In taking on the responsibility for rearing children, women stand in a different relation to the welfare state and the economy than men. Habermas (pp. 358–73), however, describes the different phases in the development of the state androgynously. He fails to appreciate that the differentiation of the economy and the state structured the power relations between men and women as well as the relations between labour and capital.

However, Fraser's conceptual framework for analysing the state draws on the classic formulation of the state's relations to women first formulated by Elizabeth Wilson. It addresses the dependence of women within the nuclear family but fails to address women's position within kinship and communal forms of social organization, which are non-individuated and communally organized.

In order to address women's position within kinship and communal forms of social organization, an emancipatory feminist project needs to adopt policies that are flexible enough to accommodate the great diversity of non-individuated socio-cultural contexts in which women live out their everyday lives. Yet the only critical standpoint of 'autonomy' that can be developed from within Wilson's theoretical framework is one which remains within the individuating logic of liberalism. This logic is universalizing. It cannot accommodate the differences that exist between women, nor the differences that exist between men and women. Women's autonomy is defined by the same standard as men's autonomy, that is, in relation to a labour market that assumes that its workers are already individuated, or at least can become individuated, equally, through the provision of state-funded services.

By grasping the emancipatory dimension of women's engagement with the state, however, it is possible to see that women's groups have been very active in attempting to 'rationalize' their lifeworld, that is to say, kinship and communal forms of social organization, in ways that attempt to accommodate diversity through a focus on the personal and particular. Ultimately, the development of these institutions will depend upon the success of a challenge mounted from a critical standpoint that attacks the very basis of the individuating logic of liberalism itself, that is, economic rationalism.

I will attempt to draw out this emancipatory dimension of women's activity using the example of women's involvement with the welfare state, then return to discuss the possible pathological consequences of a feminist politics that overlooks the way in which child-rearing activity remains embedded in non-individualized, kinship and communal forms of social organization.

Women's role in rationalizing kinship and communal forms of social organization

The historians, Lawrence Stone (1977), Eli Zaretsky (1982) and Linda Nicholson (1986), describe the construction of the bounded family as an outcome of the rise of the state. They take the view that the growth of state instrumentalities has had ambiguous effects on the power of women. On the one hand, women received some emancipation from the patriarchal and persecutory ties of communal life, but on the other hand, the increasing isolation of women in the nuclear family tended to undermine the power women were able to exert through their own kinship networks.

However, even though the positive potential for the development of the nuclear family to emancipate women from kinship and communal ties is apparent in the work of these writers, none are able to resort to an action theory which draws out women's active efforts to develop state instrumentalities to shift the burden of obligation to kin that is inherent in these forms of social organization. In other words, none of these three writers are able to envisage the bounded, nuclear family unit as something *actively* sought by women to achieve greater freedom from the confines of kinship and communal forms of social control.

Zaretsky (1982: 194) for example, still maintains the view that the nuclear family is an 'adaptation' to industrialization and the rise of the state. What remains of kinship are 'points of resistance' to the undermining of forms of social organization grounded in communal ties of human interdependence, that have managed to 'survive' the individuating effects of modernity. The implication is that the nuclear family and its relationship to kin and the local community is the result of outside forces 'whittling away' at premodern forms of social organization. The nuclear family does not appear to have been actively sought by women as part of the emancipatory project.

Yet the bounded family unit, supported by the state, does offer opportunities for the development of more voluntaristic ties between the parenting unit and their kin and local community. By taking over some of the functions previously performed by kin and the local community, state instrumentalities can reduce the parenting unit's dependence on their kin and local community. I suggest that Habermas' concept of the rationalization of the lifeworld may usefully be applied here to bring out the agency of women in transforming their social existence in such a way as to create conditions favourable for them to achieve greater autonomy, with respect to their kin and local community. The motive to create more voluntaristic ties with kin and community must have been a powerful one, consistent with the overall project of enlightenment and actively sought by many women.[12]

This view is, in fact, consistent with Zaretsky's own analysis of the origins of the welfare state in America during 1890–1920. Zaretsky clearly demonstrates the active role of women's organizations in the creation of welfare state measures that aimed to lessen all forms of interpersonal dependence. Along with the progressives, women's groups agitated for policies that would give women greater autonomy by ensuring a collective responsibility for the welfare of society's dependent members.

However, Zaretsky depicts kinship and communal ties becoming undermined as a result of the growth of the welfare state. Like most social theorists analysing modernity, forms of regulation are seen as either based on kinship and communal forms of social organization or rationalized into a form administered by the state. Instead, I take the view that both ties are still fundamental to Western society. What has changed is the form that kinship and communal ties take. Through the efforts of women to rationalize their lifeworld, kin and communal forms of social organization are now more voluntaristic, but also more dependent on interpersonal competences.

Habermas' account of the expansion of state activity depicts the rise of the welfare state only in the context of the constraints that the administrative system places on the exercise of individual autonomy. By locating women as emancipatory agents rationalizing their lifeworld, we can see that the rise of the welfare state also had some emancipatory impact, in that welfare services provide an additional organizing principle to that of kinship and community. Welfare services give women some degree of choice. It allows them some room to manoeuvre between family and state.[13]

Further, by drawing on the sociological literature relating to the maintenance of kin and communal ties, we can see that the rationalization efforts by women to replace kinship and communal forms of social organization with state administered, individuated forms of social organization did not replace so much as transform kinship and communal forms of collectivity, redistributing the burden of these forms of obligation amongst women. There is still a great deal of work involved in maintaining these ties and this work is not distributed evenly throughout the population, even amongst women. While women are still overwhelmingly responsible for maintaining kinship and communal forms of social organization, these ties are less voluntaristic where the need for communal support is the greatest; in the lower socio-economic groups and for women with preschool-age children. These women are greatly disadvantaged by the individuating logic of liberalism.

Habermas, however, seems to be unaware that certain material conditions are necessary to sustain the autonomous family unit and the autonomy of the individuals living within it. He thereby avoids the need to locate a collective political subject, committed to an agenda which might sustain the autonomy of all its citizens. A defensive strategy will do. The implication of Habermas' thesis of the colonization of the lifeworld is that if we defend our social institutions from further intrusion by the state, the dynamics of communicative action will bring about an emancipated society.

The feminist critique of Habermas' theory should at this point attempt to specify the material conditions which might sustain the autonomy of all the individuals within the family, including women. This has, of course, been central to the agenda of feminist politics since the onset of second wave feminism, but they have attempted to do this without due regard for the fact that child-rearing is embedded in kinship and communal forms of social organization which are not individuated.

These are also the areas of social life which generate normative standards for social institutions and constitute the subjectivity of individuated citizens. They may, indeed, become 'colonized' by the logic of an economic rationalist system if the critical standpoint adopted by feminists is autonomy *as defined by this system*. The material conditions for autonomy within liberalism are circumscribed by the individual's status in relation to the capitalist labour market. These individuals must already be individuated if they are to be 'free' to sell their labour power. Women whose lives are deeply embedded in kinship and communal forms of social organization are greatly disadvantaged by policies that assume that all women can be individuated equally.

The colonization of the lifeworld and feminist politics

Early second wave feminists were guided in their political agenda by the standpoint of autonomy as defined by the modernity paradigm. Within this paradigm, autonomy meant 'transcendence', mastering control over nature and the body and those forms of connectedness that tied the aspiring individual to nature and the body. Mothering was the chief obstacle inhibiting women's potential 'transcendence'. A generation of feminist scholars demonstrated convincingly how women's responsibility for the care of children was responsible for the sexual division of labour, for placing women in an economically dependent position and for inhibiting women's equal opportunity in the workplace and public life.

Mothering does indeed disadvantage women in this way within an economic rationalist system. However, what this view of emancipation occludes is any need to consider how individuals with an autonomous subjectivity are constituted. What I believe is needed here is a way of conceptualizing 'autonomy' as an act of production, that must be carried out in *concrete* action contexts by *particular* (m)others. This act of production has certain material requirements that need to be specified. Moreover, if this act of production is to be considered emancipatory for both the (m)other and child it must be reconceptualized as a relational concept, able to accommodate both the claim to autonomy of the (m)other and the claim to autonomy of the child.

However, in the political arena at present, the whole issue of child-rearing tends to become conflated with the instrumental task of child care. Although initially beneficial to the cause of women's emancipation, the feminist analysis of the political agenda for mothers appears to have stopped at this point.[14] For example, while Nancy Fraser successfully challenges Habermas' thesis on the grounds that he overlooks the need for someone to care for children, she herself does not find it necessary to analyse exactly what child-rearing practices might constitute an emancipated subjectivity. It does not appear to matter what (m)others do while they are actually performing child-rearing activity, so long as women are freed from the constraints of the normative expectations that are contained within the mothering 'role'. In this sense, Fraser remains caught in the modernity model of rationality and human agency. Child-rearing becomes an instrumental task, to be analysed like any other individuated, task-orientated activity (Fraser 1987: 45).

While Fraser's (1989: ch. 7) critical stance for assessing 'the politics of need interpretation' yields an excellent analysis of the potential for women to use the public domain to criticize the gendered aspects of our social institutions and articulate new meanings, it overlooks the need to consider the interpretive acts of women in their concrete, everyday life action contexts. Her critical standpoint overlooks the activity needed to produce individuated citizens and workers, other than that defined by the instrumental task of 'child care'. There is the danger here that child-rearing be conflated with child care and women's contribution to the constitution of an emancipated subjectivity occluded.

Moreover, Fraser appears to be suggesting that women's autonomy should depend upon the same standard as men's autonomy in the past, that is, on their relation to the capitalist labour market. But the capitalist labour market assumes that its workers are already individuated. A feminist emancipatory policy which works within the constraints of this definition of 'autonomy' must rely on the state to provide professional services previously performed by women. This strategy wrongly assumes that all women can be individuated via these services equally, as if they all carried the same caring responsibilities.

Rather than attack the economic rationalist system directly, for its inability to include non-individuated work in its accounting system, Fraser's critical standpoint ultimately gives support to the view that all socially necessary work can be individuated, through the provision of state-funded services. This solution overrides the problem of women's different circumstances and it ultimately locks the cause of women's emancipation into the terms of the capitalist labour market and its dependence upon the imperatives of continued, economic growth.

A critical standpoint dependent upon the universalizing logic of economic growth can be contrasted with one which attacks the very basis of the logic of economic growth itself.[15] This latter critical stance takes as its reference point the standpoint of women as *concrete* others. It is the standpoint of women as concrete others that is in danger of 'colonization'.

Conclusion

Early second wave feminists believed that institutions could take over all child-rearing activity and this in itself would be liberating. However, institutions which remain directly answerable to the universalizing principles of economic growth must ultimately override, or 'colonize', the standpoint of the concrete (m)other and her potential to interpret her own needs and those of her own child in the particular context she finds herself in at any particular point in time. The essence of accommodating difference lies in creating social institutions which are sensitive to the need for women as sexually specific actors to make their own judgements about their own needs in the particular socio-cultural context that they are in. To impose a rigid formula for autonomy that is defined by the logic of economic growth ultimately means undermining the potential for women as sexually specific actors to negotiate the particularities of their own situations.

This does not mean, however, that women should be left unsupported, as social dependents, to 'negotiate' the terms of their situation, where these situations involve women in grossly unequal positions of power. It is here that the standpoint of women as the generalized 'other'[16] moves into focus. The voice of the feminist generalized 'other' recognizes that social institutions need to be constructed if women are to have an autonomous voice. What is of great interest here is the way in which women, as a collective, political subject, have been engaging with the state, to 'rationalize' their lifeworld. Institutions have been created which support women's bid for autonomy, yet which are also sensitive to the need to consider women's differences, and their particular situations.

Consider, for example, the efforts made by collectives of women to set up para-state agencies that are 'community-based', for example, child-care services, family support programmes, neighbourhood centres and women's refuges. These institutions are grounded in the knowledge base of women as sexually specific actors, as 'concrete' others. This knowledge base yields critical standards.

For example, the knowledge that a child-care centre should have a staff–child ratio no higher than 1:5 has been developed from the experience of women caring for young children. This ratio is grounded in the ideal that children's individual needs should be catered for while in care. As a critical standard, it challenges the economic rationalist logic while also supporting women's efforts to achieve autonomy.

Social institutions such as family support programmes and women's refuges are also grounded in the knowledge base of women as concrete others. These institutions are guided by the ideal of helping women achieve autonomy, while recognizing the fact that their everyday lives remain embedded in kinship and communal forms of social organization. Agency workers explicitly state their goals in terms of 'empowering' women through a personal, supportive orientation that takes the particularities of each woman's situation into account. Their approach can be contrasted to the punitive, regulatory orientation of many mainstream welfare services.[17] However, their potential development, or 'rationalization', is constrained within an economic system which is unable to place any productive value on their work.

Feminist writers have some difficulty conceptualizing their relationship to these grass-roots organizations. Working within the confines of the modernity model of autonomy as 'transcendence', early second wave feminists tended to see grass-roots, or community-based organizations as supporting 'individualized' solutions to the problem of women's subordination, 'propping up' the family rather than working to change patriarchal social structures (from above). In turn, feminist activists working within these grass-roots organizations argue that academic feminists and 'femocrats' misunderstand the nature of their work. They claim that their women clients can only be 'empowered' by working through their problems with agency workers at a local and highly personal level.

The problem is that strategies for social change must take effect at two levels, at the level of the 'concrete' and the 'generalized' other. Emancipation cannot be achieved solely through imposing normative standards of 'equality' and 'autonomy' 'from above', without overriding women's differences. There is a 'politics of need interpretation' carried out at the political level, but a political agenda must consider the interpretive activity that is carried out by women as sexually specific actors, who actively reproduce norms and constitute potentially emancipatory forms of subjectivity, in their everyday life context. A feminist inspired political agenda needs to consider the basic material requirements that will give women the full benefit of communicative rationality at both these levels.

Notes

1 Mothering and feminist theory

1 Examples here include Breslow (1976), Harper and Richards (1979), Oakley (1979), Boulton (1983).

2 See Riley (1983). This standard is still used as the basis for feminist critiques of psychological models of child development. See, for example, Birns and Hay (1988) and Phoenix et al. (1991).

3 Rich (1976) made this important shift, distinguishing the potentialities of motherhood from the current institutions of motherhood. Other radical feminists such as Daly (1978) and O'Brien (1981) also developed themes which valorized women's specific experience as women.

4 For a statement of this position, see statements by the editorial collective, *Questions Feminists*, No. 1, 1977, quoted in Marks and de Courtivron (1986: 219).

5 Johnson (1988a) analyses the paradoxical implications of the work of 'difference' theorists for feminist theories of emancipation. The dilemma is also explored by Soper (1991) and Phillips (1992).

6 See, for example, Yeatman (1992).

7 This trend is illustrated by Pringle (1988), and Yeatman (1992). Ramazanoglu (1992: art. 7.4) discusses this problematic.

8 Johnson (1988a: 89) makes this point in her analysis of the dilemmas of 'difference'.

9 Lloyd (1984: 64–7) discusses the enlightenment's conception of autonomy in relation to how it excluded the 'principle of the feminine'. Lloyd (1984), Grosz (1987, 1989) and Caine and Grosz (1988) expose the dichotomous ontology of the enlightenment tradition.

10 Benhabib (1987) raises this point.

11 This is the cognitive-developmental approach to understanding 'autonomy', drawn on most recently by Habermas.

12 This is the Freudian psychoanalytical explanation of autonomy, drawn on by the early critical theorists and taken up by the exponents of the 'fatherless society' thesis, for example Mitscherlich (1973) and Lasch (1977).

13 See Lloyd (1984: 64–7) and Benhabib (1987).

14 In her critique of these studies, Adrienne Harris (1987: 40) describes how current research techniques instrumentalize the activity of infants, by attributing intentions to the infant's slightest actions.

15 See Bell (1974: 14). His rationale for this statement is his observation that 50 per cent of interactions are initiated by the child.

16 Riley (1983); Phoenix et al. (1991).

17 See, for example, Minturn and Lambert (1964) and Whiting (1977).

18 Examples here include Breslow (1976); Harper and Richards (1979); Oakley (1979); Boulton (1983); Richards (1985).

19 See, for example, Ehrenreich and English (1978); Dally (1982). Reiger's (1985) work focuses more sensitively on the contradictory effect of professional discourse on women's emancipation.

20 This is a problem succinctly identified by Pauline Johnson (1992: 2).

21 Donzelot (1980), was an important milestone here, and more recently Steedman et al. (1985) and Walkerdine and Lucey (1989).

2 Mothering and morality

1 The classic theories of socialization to which I am referring here are those of Mead (1962) and Parsons and Bales (1956). In building onto these theories, Habermas also takes on their assumptions. See, for example, his essay 'Moral development and ego identity' (1979b) where he portrays the early caregiving relationship functionally, in terms of meeting the 'concrete' needs, or 'instinctual impulses' of the child.

2 The classic example here is Kohlberg's 'Stage and sequence: the cognitive-developmental approach to socialisation', in D. Goslin (ed.) (1969), but theories derived from Freudian psychoanalysis also assume that value systems are constituted in the child after the oedipus struggle and through interaction with the father. Benjamin (1978) challenges the view that the emotions associated with nurturing, such as compassion, are natural.

3 See Firth et al. 1969; Bott 1971; Richards 1983; Richards and Salmon 1984; Segalen 1986; Finch 1989.

4 Pateman (1989) draws out this problem.

5 This is a different interpretation of Tönnies' concept of *Gemeinschaft* from Durkheim (1972: 123–40).

6 Tönnies used the term '*Wesenwille*' which has been translated as both 'essential will' and 'natural will'.

7 Cahnman (1973: 110) also draws attention to Tönnies' view that the only remedy against the undermining of nature by reason is the perfection of reason.

8 Mitzmann (1973: ch. 6) traces the roots of Tönnies' conception of *Gemeinschaft* and argues that there were no theoretical roots to Tönnies' concept of an organic community. Rather, it seemed to have been based on his memories of his own homeland and his past life, combined with the influence of the

poet, Theodore Storm, who Tönnies believed captured his poetic visions of community from his womenfolk.

9 See Tönnies in Mitzmann (1973: 106).
10 I am referring particularly here to the work of Gatens (1983, 1988); Lloyd (1984); Grosz (1987); Jones (1990); Mortimer (1990) .
11 Parsons (1973) acknowledges his debt to Tönnies. Rudolf Heberle (1973: 67) mentions Weber's acknowledgment of Tönnies' work and Cahnman (1973: 107, n. 18) writes that Tönnies also accepted Weber's categories *as* developments of his own: 'Tönnies, referring to Max Weber in *Einfuhrung*, insists that arbitrary will refers to Weber's purposive-rational action while value-rational, affectual or emotional, and traditional action, all of them although in a variety of ways, correspond to essential will.'
12 Tönnies' reference to Weber's use of his *Gemeinschaft* and *Gesellschaft* concepts supports Parsons' comments here. In note 11, I pointed out that Tönnies himself insisted that Weber's value-rational category was part of the 'essential will', that is *Gemeinschaft*. Weber, however, placed this category in 'Vergesellschaftung', corresponding to *Gesellschaft*. Weber is then only able to analyse values and morality from the point of view of the isolated individual.
13 There is a striking parallel here with the different forms of morality noted by Carol Gilligan (1982: 19) between men and women. However, I derive this difference from features of communal forms of social organization, rather than as Gilligan does from the biological make-up of men and women, although because of women's child-rearing responsibilities they are far more likely to live out their everyday lives in communal forms of social organization.
14 I have explored Habermas' assumptions here more fully in my PhD thesis, Everingham (1991).

3 The self in social theory

 1 The influence of Mead's theory can be seen in Habermas' *The Theory of Communicative Action* (1987: 33–4).
 2 Golding's essay (1982) elucidates how the psychoanalytic insights that depict the development of the psyche as the outcome of the struggle between nature and culture invariably get reduced to learning theories when adapted for sociological inquiry.
 3 I will use the masculine pronoun, as did Freud, while reviewing his theory to emphasize the fact that Freud had the psychic development of men in mind when he elaborated his theory. When he first considered the psychic development of the female, he thought it to be 'precisely analogous' (1962: 22). He believed children to be bisexual, identifying with their own sex during the oedipus struggle. For a feminist review of Freud's position, and a discussion in the light of the psychoanalytic theory of Lacan, see Mitchell and Rose (1982).
 4 Freud (1976: 402) defined 'pleasure' as connected with the 'diminution, reduction or extinction of the amounts of stimulus prevailing in the mental apparatus' and 'unpleasure' as being 'connected with their increase'.
 5 Freud (1953: 92) used the term 'primary narcissism' to denote his view that

infants were able to achieve direct satisfaction of their drives. During the early months, infants are 'auto-erotic' meaning that their instincts are not directed, or cathected, to any object in the outside world. Infants can thereby achieve direct satisfaction of their bodily needs.

6 Horner (1985) cites empirical evidence that assumptions as to early maternal-infant fusion are unfounded.

7 In his critique of Freud's Pleasure Principle, Guntrip (1969: 30) also points out that the role of the 'object', that is the mother, in determining the infant's impulses is not allowed for.

8 Although the beginning of the object-relations tradition is generally associated with the work of Melanie Klein, Harry Guntrip (1969: 204) points out that Klein still relies heavily on Instinct Theory, in particular Freud's conception of the Death Instinct which she associated with the sadistic behaviour of infants towards their mothers. Guntrip argues that this is despite Klein's findings that the child's aggression is a reaction to 'bad' object-relations. He goes on to associate the work of Fairbairn with the conscious shift in object-relations theory away from the centrality of drives.

9 Nancy Chodorow (1982) discusses the need for feminists to see these extreme, child-centred perspectives as 'a fantasy of a maternal perfectibility'.

10 For a discussion of the various schools of 'Self psychology' see Ticho (1985), Meissner (1986) and Havens (1986).

11 In addition to the articles cited in the text, see Olden (1958), Beres and Arlow (1974) and Levy (1985).

4 The study

1 In addition to the literature cited in Chapter 1, see also Grossmann et al. (1981); Main and Weston (1981); Lamb et al. (1982); Donate-Bartfield and Passman (1985); Vandell and Wilson (1987).

2 See Playgroup Association of Australia (1979: 90–1) for a short history.

3 DOCS is the major state government department concerned with social welfare.

4 I had also spent a number of years working in a voluntary capacity with Early Childhood Nurses, working from Baby Health Centres, supporting new mothers and helping to establish new playgroups.

5 Westville and Bayswater are pseudonyms for the suburbs in which the playgroups were located.

6 The TAB is a state-wide network of betting shops run by the New South Wales government.

7 The Family Day Care Programme is funded by the Federal Government and the local council. The programme provides a coordinator who selects suitable carers, matching these with families who request child care from a home base. Individual carers may care for up to four children under 5, including their own children, in their own home.

8 The NSW Health Department was responsible for the activities in the Baby Health Centre. However, the Health Department has no way of funding a child-care worker, or playgroup facilitator. This person could only have been funded by DOCS, through their Family Support Programme.

5 Maternal attitudes

1 For example, many feminists in the 1960s and 1970s criticized Bowlby's work on the grounds that he was implying that any separation from the biological mother would result in irreparable damage to the child's ability to form close relationships with other adults.
2 When questioned about alternative care arrangements, parents expressed a preference for a close relative or friend, with similar ideals and values, whom they could 'trust'. The regulations for day-care facilities are also based on the idea that carers should be able to give consistency and continuity of care to young children.
3 For accounts of child-rearing in New Age communes see Abrams and McCulloch (1976); Berger (1981); Munro-Clark (1986).
4 Ann Dally (1982: 80) describes the development of these scheduling techniques as a result of the influence of Truby King. Ehrenreich and English (1978: 85) describe the development of scheduling techniques as an outcome of attempts by psychologists to bring children up 'scientifically'; the aim being to eliminate the irrational and emotional elements in the mother–infant relationship and thereby create a more disciplined workforce. Kerreen Reiger (1985) draws out the contradictory nature of this scientific approach, pointing out that this approach at least undermined the assumption that mothering was 'natural'.
5 Kohlberg, for example, regards attitudes towards love and care as 'private' activity, which he then locates outside the the legitimate domain of moral analysis. Benhabib (1987: 82) quotes Kohlberg's 'definition of the domain of *special relationships of obligation*' as follows: 'the spheres of kinship, love, friendship, and sex that elicit considerations of care are usually understood to be spheres of personal decision-making as are, for instance, the problems of marriage and divorce'.
6 Elshtain (1982) also discusses the way in which women's mothering activity has been conceptualized as occurring in a 'private' space, as opposed to the public world. She also suggests that mothering occurs in a social space, from which base they need to be able to publicly articulate their common concerns as mothers.

6 Taking the attitude of the child

1 I use 'mother' rather than 'carer' to describe aspects of the dyad's interaction which were specific to the primary carer. Children did not try to assert themselves with carer's who were only minding them for brief periods, although they did seek out their carer for comfort if they were upset.
2 There is an interesting comparison to make here with the way in which adults in the Aboriginal settlement studied by Annette Hamilton (1981) discouraged the 6–18 month-old children from wandering away and exploring. Adults presented the environment away fom the camp as a fearful place of 'debil-debils' and always returned young children to their mothers if they began to wander away. The alternative children, on the other hand, enjoyed great freedom on these outings, protected by adults who were prepared to follow.
3 Carers who were looking after another mother's child at playgroup treated the

child in the same manner as their own. Most often the child would be a similar age to their own child and the mother would be guided in her behaviour towards the child by the same set of expectations that she had built through caring for her own child.

4 According to a report on baby health services carried out in the Hunter Region, New South Wales in 1980, mothers attend baby health centres on the basis of the particular personality of the early childhood nurse. Supportive and empathetic nurses are greatly favoured over dogmatic advice givers and this factor largely determines which clinics are visited by mothers (New South Wales Health Department, Hunter Region 1980).

5 Breast-feeding infants in this manner is recommended by the Nursing Mothers Association as a way of ensuring an adequate milk supply. The supply of milk is directly related to the amount of breast stimulation. In many cases, a four-hourly feeding regime does not give the breast sufficient stimulation for successful breast-feeding.

7 Maternal attitudes and maternal-infant conflict

1 Although these same patterns could be produced by an alternative primary carer, I use 'mother' in this chapter in order to differentiate the different interactive patterns of mothers and other carers who attended playgroup. I also wish to distinguish between the different orientation of the mothers and the fathers.

2 Klein (1987: ch. 1) describes the way in which intensely experienced effects become imprinted into the neuro-physiological system of the child.

3 The object-relations psychoanalyst, Winnicott (1965: 73–82) theorizes the origins of 'the capacity to be concerned'. He uses this notion to denote the 'positive' dimension of the guilt complex. He also locates its origins 'in the infant–mother relationship, when already the infant is an established unit, and when the infant feels the mother, or mother-figure, to be a whole person'. However, Winnicott's analysis of the development of this crucial, psychological configuration is limited by his action theoretical tools. Thus, he can only describe the maternal-infant relationship in terms of the 'good-enough mothering' model that I discussed in Chapter 3. Although he states that the development of the capacity of concern for another 'cannot be thought of in any way but as an achievement', he is unable to analyse the mother's active contribution to its achievement, nor the normative context in which this occurs.

8 The politics of the particular and the generalized 'other'

1 Feminist analyses of the separation of the public and private realms of social life by the early contract theorists are summarized by Pateman (1989). Nicholson (1986) gives an account of Locke's creation of the autonomous individual through the construction of the public and private domains as separate and distinct spheres of social activity. Elshtain (1981) discusses how this separation silenced the collective concerns of women.

2 Feminist writing on the welfare state describes women's responsibilities for the care of society's dependent members as the immediate cause of women's disadvantaged position in the workforce and the 'feminization of poverty'. See Baldock and Cass (1983: Introduction).

3 See Kandall (1989: 136).

4 I have based this summary of Horkheimmer's thesis on Benjamin's (1978) analysis of the Frankfurt School's conception of autonomy.

5 Jessica Benjamin (1978) analyses this argument as elaborated by the Frankfurt School. Habermas (1985a) also discusses this theme. Joel Whitebook (1985) points out that the thesis that authoritarian socialization is the only path, or even *a* path to autonomy, can be contested.

6 Whitebook (1985: 147) discusses this aporia.

7 Formal child care services need to be seen as performing a supportive service for parents; a supplement to parenting rather than a replacement for parenting. Child-rearing as distinct from child care must still be performed by parents who need personal contact with other parents and children if they are to participate directly in the mothering culture and the definition of the norms that guide child-rearing activity. Working mothers in my study expressed the view that contact with other mothers and children was still a necessary dimension of their child-rearing activity, even though returning to a paid work environment often helped them to overcome their own social isolation.

8 Habermas (1987: 342) discusses the positive potential of modernity with respect to the process of individuation when he points out how Marx's theory of value considered only the negative aspect of modernity, that is, reification and not the positive aspect of modernity, that is, individuation. According to Habermas, this was because Marx could not distinguish between reification and the structural differentiation of the lifeworld.

9 This is a phrase used by Whitebook (1985: 147) when discussing the dilemmas of the Frankfurt philosophers.

10 See Stone (1977: 124).

11 See Firth et al. (1969); Bott (1971); Richards and Salmon (1984).

12 Stone (1977: 93) describes the persecutory forms of regulation characteristic of forms of communal organization common to Western society before the expansion of the state. These forms of regulation must have been just as repressive for women as for men.

13 Linda Gordon (1986) draws out the way women are sometimes able to use welfare services against patriarchal kinship relations.

14 See Franzway et al. (1989: 63).

15 See, for example, Waring (1988).

16 I have co-opted the terms 'the generalized other' and 'the concrete other' from Benhabib (1987).

17 See the interviews with agency workers in Bullen (1989). Humphries (1982) argues that working-class women prefer informal systems of care because they can retain more control over these systems.

Bibliography

Abrams, P. and McCulloch, A. (1976) *Communes, Sociology and Society.* London, Cambridge University Press.

Ainsworth, M. (1977a) 'Attachment theory and its utility in cross-cultural research'. In P. Leiderman, S. Tulkin and A. Rosenfeld (eds) *Culture and Infancy: Variations in Human Experience.* New York, Academic Press.

Ainsworth, M. (1977b) 'Infant development and mother–infant interaction among Gandan and American Families'. In P. Leiderman, S. Tulkin and A. Rosenfeld (eds) *Culture and Infancy: Variations in Human Experience.* New York, Academic Press.

Alford, C.F. (1987) 'Habermas, post-Freudian psychoanalysis, and the end of the individual', *Theory and Society*, 16, 3–29.

Alford, C.F. (1990) 'Reason and reparation: a Kleinian account of the critique of instrumental reason', *Theory and Society*, 19, 37–61.

Baldock, C. and Cass, B. (1983) *Women, Welfare and the State.* Sydney, Allen and Unwin.

Barrett, M. and McIntosh, M. (1982) *The Anti-Social Family.* London, Thetford.

Basch, M. (1983) 'Empathetic understanding: a review of the concept and some theoretical considerations, *Journal American Psychoanalytic Association*, 31, 101–26.

Bell, R. (1974) 'Contribution of Human Infants to Caregiving and Social Interaction'. In L. Lewis and S. Rosenblum (eds) *The Effect of the Infant on its Caregiver.* New York, John Wiley.

Benhabib, S. (1987) 'The generalized and the concrete other'. In S. Benhabib and D. Cornell (eds) *Feminism as Critique.* Oxford, Praxis International.

Benjamin, J. (1978) 'Authority and the family revisited: or a world without fathers?', *New German Critique*, 13, 35–57.

Benjamin, J. (1981) 'The Oedipal riddle: authority, and the new narcissism'. In J. Diggins and M. Kamm (eds) *The Problem of Authority in America*. Philadelphia, Temple.

Benjamin, J. (1990) *The Bonds of Love*. London, Virago.

Beres, D. and Arlow, J. (1974) 'Fantasy and identification in empathy', *Psychoanalytic Quarterly*, 43, 26–48.

Berger, B. (1981) *The Survival of a Counterculture*. Berkeley, University of California Press.

Bettelheim, B. (1969) *Children of the Dream*. London, Paladin.

Bettelheim, B. (1987) *A Good Enough Parent: The Guide to Bringing Up Your Child*. London, Thames and Hudson.

Birns, B. and Hay, D. (eds) (1988) *The Different Faces of Motherhood*. New York and London, Plenum.

Bott, E. (1971) *Family and Social Network*. New York, Free Press.

Boulton, M. (1983) *On Being a Mother: A Study of Women with Pre-school Children*. London, Tavistock.

Bowlby, J. (1963) *Child Care and the Growth of Love*. Harmondsworth, Pelican.

Brand, A. (1990) *The Force of Reason*. Sydney, Allen and Unwin.

Brazelton, T. (1974) 'The origins of reciprocity'. In M. Lewis and S. Rosenblum (eds) *The Effect of the Infant on its Caregiver*. New York, John Wiley.

Brazelton, T. (1977) 'Implications of infant development among the Mayan Indians of Mexico'. In P. Leiderman, S. Tulkin and A. Rosenfeld (eds) *Culture and Infancy: Variations in Human Experience*. London, Academic Press.

Breslow, L. (1976) *Worlds of Pain: Life in the Working Class Family*. New York, Basic Books.

Buie, D. (1981) 'Empathy: its nature and limitations', *Journal of the American Psychoanalytic Association*, 29, 281–307.

Bullen, P. (1989) *Family Support Services in New South Wales*. Sydney, Community Publishing.

Cahnman, W.J. (ed.) (1973) *Ferdinand Tönnies: A New Evaluation*. Leiden, E.J. Brill.

Caine, B. and Grosz, L. (1988) *Crossing Boundaries*. Sydney, Allen and Unwin.

Chodorow, N. (1978) *The Reproduction of Mothering: Psychoanalysis and the Sociology of Gender*. London, University of California.

Chodorow, N. (1982) 'The fantasy of the perfect mother'. In B. Thorne and M. Yalom (eds) *Rethinking the Family*. New York, Longman.

Chodorow, N. (1985) 'Beyond drive theory. Object relations and the limits of radical individualism', *Theory and Society*, 14, 271–319.

Curthoys, A. (1988) *For and Against Feminism: A Personal Journey into Feminist Theory and History*. Sydney, Allen and Unwin.

Dally, A. (1982) *Inventing Motherhood*. London, Burnett Books.

Daly, M. (1978) *Gyn/Ecology: the Metaethics of Radical Feminism*. London, Women's Press.

Department of Health, New South Wales (1983) *Our Babies*.

Dews, P. (ed.) (1986) *Jürgen Habermas: Autonomy and Solidarity. Interviews*. London, Verso.

Donate-Bartfield, E. and Passman, R. (1985) 'Attentiveness of mothers and fathers to their baby's cries', *Infant Behavior and Development*, 8, 385–93.

Donzelot, J. (1980) *The Policing of Families*. London, Hutchinson.

Durkheim, E. (1972) *Selected Writings*. A. Giddens (ed.). Cambridge, University of Chicago Press.

Ehrenreich, B. and English, D. (1978) *For Her Own Good; 150 Years of Expert Advice to Women*. London, Pluto.

Elshtain, J.B. (1981) *Public Man, Private Woman: Woman in Social and Political Thought*. Princeton, Princeton University Press.

Elshtain, J.B. (1982) ' "Thank heaven for little girls": the dialectics of development'. In J.B. Elshtain (ed.) *The Family in Political Thought*. Lewes, Sussex, Harvester Press.

Elshtain, J.B. (1983) 'Antigone's daughters: reflections on female identity and the state'. In I. Diamond (ed.) *Families, Politics, and Public Policy: a Feminist Dialogue on Women and the State*. New York, Longman.

Everingham, C. (1991) Motherhood and Modernity: An Investigation into the Rational Dimension of Mothering. Unpublished PhD thesis, University of Newcastle.

Ferguson, K. (1984) *The Feminist Case Against Bureaucracy*. Philadelphia, Temple University Press.

Finch, J. (1989) *Family Obligations and Social Change*. Cambridge, Polity Press.

Firth, R., Hubert, J. and Forge, A. (1969) *Families and their Relatives*. London, Routledge and Kegan Paul.

Franzway, S., Court, D. and Connell, R. (1989) *Staking a Claim: Feminism, Bureaucracy and the State*. Sydney, Allen and Unwin.

Fraser, N. (1987) 'What's critical about critical theory? The case of Habermas and Gender'. In S. Benhabib and D. Cornell (eds) *Feminism as Critique*. Cambridge, Polity Press.

Fraser, N. (1989) 'Women, welfare and the politics of need interpretation'. In N. Fraser (ed.) *Unruly Practices: Power, Discourse and Gender in Contemporary Social Theory*. Cambridge, Polity Press.

Freud, S. (1950) *Beyond the Pleasure Principle*. London, Hogarth Press.

Freud, S. (1953) 'Group psychology and the analysis of the ego'. In J. Rickmann (ed.) *A General Selection from the Works of S. Freud*. London, Hogarth Press.

Freud, S. (1962) *The Ego and the Id*. London, Hogarth Press.

Freud, S. (1973) *Civilization and its Discontents*. London, Hogarth Press.

Freud, S. (1976) *Introductory Lectures on Psychoanalysis*. Harmondsworth, Penguin.

Gatens, M. (1983) 'A critique of the sex–gender distinction'. In J. Allen and P. Patton (eds) *Beyond Marxism? Interventions After Marx.* Sydney, Intervention Publications.

Gatens, M. (1988) 'Towards a feminist philosophy of the body'. In B. Caine and E. Grosz (eds) *Crossing Boundaries.* Sydney, Allen and Unwin.

Gerth, H. and Wright Mills, C. (eds) (1977) *From Max Weber: Essays in Sociology.* London, Routledge and Kegan Paul.

Gilligan, C. (1982) *In a Different Voice; Psychological Theory and Women's Development.* London, Harvard University Press.

Glaser, B. and Strauss, A. (1970) 'Theoretical sampling'. In N. Denzin (ed.) *Sociological Methods.* Chicago, Aldine.

Golding, R. (1982) 'Freud, psychoanalysis, and sociology: some observations on the sociological analysis of the individual', *British Journal of Sociology*, 33, 545–62.

Gordon, L. (1986) 'Family violence, feminism and social control', *Feminist Studies*, 12, 453–78.

Goslin, D. (ed.) (1969) *Handbook of Socialisation: Theory and Research.* Chicago, Rand McNally.

Green, C. (1984) *Toddler Taming: a Parent's Guide to (Surviving) the First Four Years.* Sydney, Doubleday.

Grossmann, K. and K., Huber, F. and Wartner, U. (1981) 'German children's behavior towards their mothers at 12 months and their fathers at 18 months in Ainsworth's strange situation', *International Journal of Behavioral Development*, 4, 157–81.

Grosz, E. (1987) 'Notes towards a corporeal feminism', *Australian Feminist Studies*, 5, 1–16.

Grosz, E. (1989) *Sexual Subversions.* Sydney, Allen and Unwin.

Guntrip, H. (1969) *Personality Structure and Human Interaction.* New York, International University Press.

Haas, L. (1982) 'Parental sharing of childcare tasks in Sweden', *Journal of Family Issues*, 3, 389–412.

Habermas, J. (1976) *Legitimation Crisis.* London, Heinemann.

Habermas, J. (1979a) *Communication and the Evolution of Society.* T. McCarthy (trans. and ed.). London, Heinemann.

Habermas, J. (1979b) 'Moral development and ego identity'. In J. Habermas. *Communication and the Evolution of Society.* T. McCarthy (trans. and ed.). London, Heinemann.

Habermas, J. (1979c) 'Toward a reconstruction of historical materialism'. In J. Habermas. *Communication and the Evolution of Society.* T. McCarthy (trans. and ed.). London, Heinemann.

Habermas, J. (1982) 'A reply to my critics'. In J.B. Thompson and D. Held (eds) *Habermas Critical Debates.* London, Macmillan.

Habermas, J. (1984) *The Theory of Communicative Action 1: Reason and the Rationalisation of Society.* Boston, Beacon Press.

Habermas, J. (1985a) 'Psychic thermidor and the rebirth of rebellious subjectivity'. In R. Bernstein (ed.) *Habermas and Modernity*. Cambridge, Polity Press.

Habermas, J. (1985b) 'Remarks on the concept of communicative action'. In G. Seebass and R. Tuomela (eds) *Social Action*. Dordrecht, Holland, Reidel.

Habermas, J. (1987) *The Theory of Communicative Action 2: Lifeworld and System: A Critique of Functionalist Reason*. Cambridge, Polity Press.

Hamilton, A. (1981) *Nature and Nurture; Aboriginal Child-Rearing in North-Central Arnhem Land*. Canberra, Australian Institute of Aboriginal Studies.

Harper, J. and Richards, L. (1979) *Mothers and Working Mothers*. Harmondsworth, Penguin.

Harris, A. (1987) 'The rationalization of infancy'. In J. Broughton (ed.) *Critical Theories of Psychological Development*. New York, Path.

Havens, L. (1986) 'A theoretical basis for the conception of self and authentic self', *Journal American Psychoanalytic Association*, 34, 363–78.

Heberle, R. (1973) 'Three aspects of the sociology of Tönnies'. In W. Cahnmann (ed.) *Ferdinand Tönnies: A New Evaluation*. Leiden, E.J. Brill.

Horner, T. (1985) 'The psychic life of the young infant: review and critique of the psychoanalytic concepts of symbiosis and infantile omnipotence', *American Journal of Orthopsychiatry*, 85, 324–43.

Humphries, J. (1982) 'The working class family: a Marxist perspective'. In J. Elshtain (ed.) *The Family in Political Thought*. Lewes, Sussex, Harvester Press.

Hwang, C. (1986) 'Behavior of Swedish primary and secondary caretaking fathers in relation to mother's presence', *Developmental Psychology*, 22, 749–51.

Johnson, P. (1988a) 'Feminism and difference; the dilemmas of Luce Irigaray', *Australian Feminist Studies*, 6, 87–96.

Johnson, P. (1988b) 'More on the Socialism in Socialist Feminism: a Response to Pringle', *Australian Feminist Studies*, 7 and 8, 179–86.

Johnson, P. (1992) 'Feminism and liberalism', *Australian Feminist Studies*, 14, 57–68.

Jones, K. (1990) 'Citizenship in a woman-friendly polity', *Signs*, 15, 781–812.

Kandall, T. (1989) *The Woman Question in Classical Sociological Theory*. Miami, Florida International University Press.

Klein, J. (1987) *Our Need for Others and its Roots in Infancy*. London and New York, Tavistock.

Kohlberg, L. (1969) 'Stage and sequence: the cognitive-developmental approach to socialisation'. In D. Goslin (ed.) *Handbook of Socialisation: Theory and Research*. Chicago, Rand McNally.

Kohut, H. (1983) *The Restoration of the Self*. New York, International Universities Press.

Lamb, M., Hwang, C., Frodi, A. and M. (1982) 'Security of mother– and father–infant attachment and its relation to sociability with strangers in traditional and nontraditional Swedish families', *Infant Behavior*, 5, 355–67.

Lasch, C. (1977) *Haven in a Heartless World: The Family Besieged*. New York, Basic Books.

Lasch, C. (1978) *The Culture of Narcissism*. New York, W.W. Norton.

Laslett, P. (1972) *Household and Family in Past Time*. London, Cambridge University Press.

Levy, S. (1985) 'Empathy and psychoanalytic technique', *Journal of the American Psychoanalytic Association*, 33, 353–79.

Lewis, M. and Lee-Painter, S. (1974) 'An interactionist approach to the mother–infant dyad'. In M. Lewis and S. Rosenblum (eds) *The Effect of the Infant on its Caregiver*. New York, John Wiley.

Lloyd, G. (1984) *The Man of Reason: 'Male' and 'Female' in Western Philosophy*. London, Methuen.

Lloyd, G. (1985) 'Masters, slaves and others'. In R. Edgley and O. Osborne (eds) *Radical Philosophy*. London, Verso.

Main, M. and Weston, D. (1981) 'The quality of toddler's relationship to mother and father: related to conflict behavior and the readiness to establish new relationships', *Child Development*, 52, 932–40.

Malinowski, B. (1963) *The Family Among the Australian Aborigines*. New York, Schocken Books.

Marks, E. and de Courtivron, I. (1981) *New French Feminisms: An Anthology*. Lewes, Sussex, Harvester Press.

Martin, B. (1981) *A Sociology of Contemporary Cultural Change*. Oxford, Basil Blackwell.

Mead, G.H. (1962) *The Social Psychology of George Herbert Mead*. A. Strauss (ed.). Chicago, Phoenix.

Mead, M. and Wolfenstein, M. (1955) *Childhood in Contemporary Cultures*. Chicago, University of Chicago Press.

Meissner, W. (1986) 'Can psychoanalysis find its self?', *Journal of the American Psychoanalytic Association*, 34, 379–99.

Minturn, L. and Lambert, W. (1964) *Mothers of Six Cultures: Antecedents of Child-Rearing*. New York, John Wiley.

Mitchell, J. and Rose, J. (eds) (1982) *Feminine Sexuality: Jaques Lacan and the Ecole Freudienne*. London, Macmillan.

Mitscherlich, A. (1973) *Society Without the Father*. New York, J. Aronson.

Mitzmann, A. (1973) *Sociology and Estrangement*. New York, Alfred A. Knopf.

Mortimer, L. (1990) 'What if I talked like a woman right here in public', *Arena*, 92, 43–63.

Munro-Clark, M. (1986) *Communes in Rural Australia: The Movement Since 1970*. Sydney, Hale and Iremonger.

Nelson, M. (1990) 'Mothering others' children: the experiences of family day-care providers', *Signs*, 15, 586–685.

New South Wales Department of Health (1983) *Our Babies*. Sydney, NSW Department of Health.

New South Wales Health Department, Hunter Region (1980) *Report of the Baby Health Services Review Committee*. Newcastle, NSW Department of Health, unpublished.

Newson, J. and Newson, E. (1966) *Patterns of Infant Care in an Urban Community*. Harmondsworth, Penguin.

Nicholson, L. (1986) *The Limits of Social Theory in the Age of the Family*. New York, Columbia University Press.

Oakley, A. (1979) *Becoming a Mother*. Oxford, Martin Robertson.

O'Brien, M. (1981) *The Politics of Reproduction*. London, Routledge and Kegan Paul.

Olden, C. (1958) 'Notes on the development of empathy', *The Psychoanalytic Study of the Child*, Vol. XIII, 505–18.

Parsons, T. (1951) 'Categories of the orientation and organization of action'. In T. Parsons and E. Shils (eds) *Toward a General Theory of Action*. Cambridge, Harvard University Press.

Parsons, T. (1973) 'A Note on Gemeinschaft and Geschellschaft'. In W. Cahnmann (ed.) *Ferdinand Tönnies: A New Evaluation*. Leiden, E.J. Brill.

Parsons, T. and Bales, R. (1956) *Family, Socialization and Interaction Process*. London, Routledge and Kegan Paul.

Pateman, C. (1989) 'Feminist critiques of the public/private dichotomy'. In C. Pateman (ed.) *The Disorder of Women*. Cambridge, Polity Press.

Pedersen, F. (1980) *The Father–Infant Relationship*. New York, Praeger.

Phillips, A. (1992) 'Feminism, Equality and Difference'. In L. McDowell and R. Pringle (eds) *Defining Women*. Cambridge, Polity Press.

Phoenix, A., Woollett, A. and Lloyd, E. (eds) (1991) *Motherhood: Meanings, Practices and Ideologies*. London, Sage.

Playgroup Association of Australia (1979) *Fun at Playgroup. A Book About Playgroups in Australia*. Belconnen, Playgroup Association of Australia.

Pringle, R. (1988) ' "Socialist-feminism" in the eighties: reply to Curthoys', *Australian Feminist Studies*, 6, 25–30.

Ramazanoglu, C. (1992) 'Feminism and liberation'. In L. McDowell and R. Pringle (eds) *Defining Women*. Cambridge, Polity Press.

Reiger, K. (1985) *The Disenchantment of the Home; Modernizing the Australian Family 1880–1940*. Melbourne, Oxford University Press.

Rich, A. (1976) *Of Woman Born: Motherhood as Experience and Institution*. New York, Norton.

Richards, L. (1983) Families in a Suburb: Network Management and its Varied Results. Working Paper No. 64, Department of Sociology, La Trobe University, Victoria.

Richards, L. (1985) *Having Families*. Harmondsworth, Penguin.

Richards, L. and Salmon, J. (1984) There When You Need Them: Family Life Stage and Social Network. Working Paper No. 68, Department of Sociology, La Trobe University, Victoria.

Riley, D. (1983) *War in the Nursery: Theories of the Child and Mother*. London, Virago.

Ruddick, S. (1982) 'Maternal thinking'. In B. Thorne and M. Yalom (eds) *Rethinking the Family*. New York and London, Longman.

Rutter, M. (1981) *Maternal Deprivation Reassessed*. Harmondsworth, Penguin.

Salomon, A. (1973) 'In Memoriam Ferdinand Tönnies'. In W. Cahnman (ed.) *Ferdinand Tönnies: A New Evaluation*. Leiden, E.J. Brill.

Schaffer, R. (1977) *Mothering*. Glasgow, William Collins.

Schaffer, R. and Dunn, J. (eds) (1979) *The First Year of Life; Psychological and Medical Implications of Early Experience*. Chichester, John Wiley.

Scheper-Hughes, N. (1985) 'Culture, scarcity and maternal thinking: maternal detachment and infant survival in a Brazilian shantytown', *Ethos*, 4, 291–317.

Schutz, A. (1970) *On Phenomenology and Social Relations*. Chicago, University of Chicago.

Segal, H. (1979) *Klein*. Lewes, Sussex, Harvester Press.

Segalen, M. (1986) *Historical Anthropology of the Family*. Cambridge, Cambridge University Press.

Siim, B. (1985) 'Towards a feminist rethinking of the welfare state'. In K. Jones and A. Jonasdothir (eds) *The Political Interests of Gender: Developing Theory and Research With a Feminist Face*. London, Sage.

Soper, K. (1991) 'Postmodernism and its discontents', *Feminist Review*, 39, 97–108.

Steedman, C., Urwin, C. and Walkerdine, V. (eds) (1985) *Language, Gender and Childhood*. London, Routledge and Kegan Paul.

Stern, D. (1974) 'Mother and infant at play'. In M. Lewis and S. Rosenblum (eds) *The Effect of the Infant on its Caregiver*. New York, John Wiley.

Sternglanz, S. and Nash, A. (1988) 'Ethological contributions to the study of human motherhood'. In B. Birns and D. Hay (eds) *The Different Faces of Motherhood*. New York and London, Plenum.

Stone, L. (1977) *The Family, Sex and Marriage in England 1500–1800*. London, Weidenfeld and Nicolson.

Ticho, E. (1985) 'The alternate schools and the self', *Journal of the American Psychoanalytic Association*, 33, 849–91.

Tiger, L. and Shepher, J. (1975) *Women in the Kibbutz*. New York, Harcourt Brace Jovanovich.

Tönnies, F. (1957) *Community and Society*. C. Loomis (trans. and ed.). New York, Harper and Row.

Tönnies, F. (1973) 'End and means in social life'. In W. Cahnman (ed.) *Ferdinand Tönnies: A New Evaluation*. Leiden, E.J. Brill.

Trebilcot, J. (1984) *Mothering: Essays in Feminist Theory*. Totowa, Rowman and Allanheld.

Urwin, C. (1984) 'Power relations in the emergence of language'. In J.

Henriques, W. Hollway, C. Urwin, C. Venn and V. Walkerdine (eds) *Changing the Subject*. London, Methuen.

Vandell, D. and Wilson, K. (1987) 'Infants' interactions with mother, sibling, and peer: contrasts and relations between interaction systems', *Child Development*, 58, 176–86.

Walkerdine, V. and Lucey, H. (1989) *Democracy in the Kitchen: Regulating Mothers and Socialising Daughters*. London, Virago.

Waring, M. (1988) *Counting for Nothing: What Men Value and What Women are Worth*. Sydney, Allen and Unwin.

Wearing, B. (1984) *The Ideology of Motherhood*. Sydney, George Allen and Unwin.

Weber, M. (1958) *The Protestant Ethic and the Spirit of Capitalism*. New York, Charles Scribner.

Weber, M. (1968) *Economy and Society*. New York, Bedminster.

Wellmer, A. (1985) 'Reason, utopia, and the dialectic of enlightenment'. In R. Bernstein (ed.) *Habermas and Modernity*. Cambridge, Polity Press.

Whitebook, J. (1985) 'Reason and happiness: some psychoanalytic themes in critical theory'. In R. Bernstein (ed.) *Habermas and Modernity*. Cambridge, Polity Press.

Whiting, J. (1977) 'Psychocultural research'. In P. Leiderman, S. Tulkin and A. Rosenfeld (eds) *Culture and Infancy: Variations in the Human Experience*. London, Academic Press.

Winnicott, D. (1965) *The Maturational Processes and the Facilitating Environment*. London, Hogarth Press.

Yeatman, A. (1992) 'Postmodernity and revisioning the political', *Social Analysis*, 30, 116–30.

Young, M. and Willmott, P. (1962) *Family and Kinship in East London*. Harmondsworth, Penguin.

Zaretsky, E. (1976) *Capitalism, the Family and Personal Life*. London, Pluto.

Zaretsky, E. (1982) 'The place of the family in the origins of the welfare state'. In B. Thorne and M. Yalom (eds) *Rethinking the Family*. London, Longman.

Index

action
  in dyad, 69, 95, 98, 100–3, 106
  frameworks, 7, 9, 23–30, 35,
    45–6, 127, 130
  spheres of, 8, 28, 83, 123–4,
    133
  see also disciplinary action
agency
  and autonomy, 120–1
  of child, 8, 10, 17, 36, 70, 85, 89,
    93, 125
  modernist conception of, 14, 133
  of mother, 15, 121, 125
  political, 126
  spheres of, 6–7, 124–5
  of women, 6, 8, 17, 131
Ainsworth, M., 98
Alford, F., 115
association, 23–4, 27
  forms of social organization,
    28–9, 84, 124, 128
  see also Gesellschaft
attachment, 9, 12, 35, 98, 104, 105
attitudes
  as care-giving orientation, 86–9
    passim, 96, 114
  construction of, 83, 92, 95, 115
  maternal, 71, 75–7, 79, 81, 87,
    99–100

and mother's autonomy, 115, 123,
    124
  as social orientation, 27–32, 123,
    128
authenticity, 120–2
authority, 18, 104, 109, 120–3
autonomy
  competing claims to, 29, 115, 122
  constitution of, 18, 33, 36, 42–3,
    122
  as critical standard, 14–16, 129,
    132
  in critical theory, 120
  as feminist objective, 3, 6, 11
  material basis for, 29, 128, 132
  as relational concept, 6, 8, 15, 33,
    120–1, 133
  as societal ideal, 6, 8, 33, 68, 70,
    124, 134–5
  women's, 11, 18, 32–3, 93,
    115–16, 121, 123, 129–35
    passim

Barrett, M., 122
Basch, M., 45
Bell, R., 9, 68, 86
Benjamin, J., 18–19, 42, 46, 121,
    122, 123
Berger, B., 68

Birns, B., 10
bottle
 and infant feeding, 65, 77, 78, 85,
  90, 91, 96
Bowlby, J., 9
Brazelton, T., 9, 86
breast
 and infant feeding, 65, 67, 70, 73,
  80, 91, 93, 94, 112
Buie, D., 45

care
 alternative, 104–5
 shared, 65, 68
 shared parenting, 65–6
 see also child care, diffuse care-
  giving, surrogate care
care-giving
 behaviour, 9, 13, 68, 70, 91,
  93–4, 98
 diffuse, 106
 relationship, 68–71, 75, 94–5, 101,
  107
child care, 14–15, 122, 133–4
 workers, 50, 53
child-centred, 92, 95–7, 103, 104
 see also child-rearing ideals
child development, 16, 33
child-rearing
 advice, 34, 72–3, 79, 90
 cross-cultural, 12, 68, 70
 ideals, 10–11, 17, 44, 60, 77, 83,
  89, 91, 95, 124–5
 practices, 33, 67, 79, 82, 98, 106,
  129
 and social space, 81, 124, 126,
  128, 130, 132
 and subjectivity of child, 133
 women's responsibility, 119, 122,
  124, 133
 see also care-giving
Chodorow, N., 18, 46, 122
citizen, 119, 132, 133
communal
 action, 23, 28, 83, 124
 care, 66, 68
 forms of social organization, 25–32
  passim, 83–4, 123, 126–32
  passim
 support, 81

standards for care, 79
 see also Gemeinschaft
communicative action, 18, 121, 122,
 126–9, 132
community, 23–6, 35, 70, 130–1
 groups, 50, 51
 need for, 79, 81
 services, 55, 134–5
 worker, 55–7
connectedness, 38–44 *passim*, 122,
 132
critical
 theory, 115, 120–1
 standard, 134–5
 standpoint, 129–34 *passim*

Dally, A., 73
demand feeding, 73, 77–8, 89–93,
 95
dependence
 interdependence, 24, 130
 interpersonal, 23, 28, 29, 79
 of women, 129, 132, 134
dichotomous categories, 5–6, 12, 17,
 24, 25–6, 28, 34, 122, 124
discipline, 110–11, 114
 disciplinary action, 99–103, 106
drive theory, 40, 43–4, 46
Dunn, J., 10, 68, 93
dyad
 studies of, 9, 21–2, 68, 86
 interaction in, 46, 93, 97, 99,
  103

economic, 125, 127, 128, 135
 rationalism, 130, 132–3, 135
economy, 116, 127, 129
Elshtain, J., 125
emancipation
 men's, 6
 as societal goal, 119–20, 132
 strategies for women's, 4–5, 124,
  134–5
emancipatory
 project, 126, 129–31, 133, 135
 struggles of women, 14, 130
empathy, 44–5, 80–1
enlightenment, 5–6, 116, 131
ethics, 4, 25, 33
equality, 3, 125

family day care, 54, 104
family support service, 50–1, 55,
  134–5
fathers, 56, 64–5, 81, 105–6
  as primary carer, 66
  role, 21–2
feminism, 3–4, 10, 13, 18, 132
feminist
  perspectives on mothering and the
    family, 7, 22, 122, 126–8
  political strategies, 8, 15, 124,
    130–5 *passim*
  value system, 33
Foucault, M., 4, 15, 16
Frankfurt philosophers, 120, 127
Fraser, N., 128–9, 133
Freud, S., 37–42, 120

Gemeinschaft, 23–9
gender, 62, 83, 126, 129, 133
Gesellschaft, 23–7
Glaser, B., 51
good-enough mothering, 11–12, 42,
  73
Green, C., 73
Guntrip, H., 11, 41

Haas, L., 66
Habermas, J., 17–18, 26, 29, 31, 46,
  116, 121–2, 125–9, 131–3
Hale, D., 10
Hamilton, A., 13
Horkheimmer, M., 120, 121
Hwang, C., 66

individualism, 3, 93, 119
individuation, 36, 42, 119, 122,
  124–7, 129–33
  see also autonomy
instrumental action, 30
  and nurturing, 9–10, 20–2, 35,
    41, 42, 70, 95, 129, 133
  as father's role, 21–2

King, T., 73
kinship, 23, 128–32
Klein, M., 40–1, 44
Kohut, H., 18, 42–4, 95, 122

Lamb, M., 66, 69
Lasch, C., 121, 127
Lee-Painter, S., 68
liberalism, 119, 120, 124–5,
  129–30, 132
Locke, J., 124
Lucey, H., 15–17

Malinowski, B., 13
Martin, B., 73
McIntosh, M., 122
Mead, G.H., 32–7, 39, 121, 122
Mead, M., 12
meanings, 34–5, 89, 124, 133
Mitscherlich, A., 121
Mitzmann, A., 25
moral, 26, 78
  attitudes, 29–30, 32, 115, 123
  development, 36, 38–40, 79
  dimension of social life, 27–8, 31,
    83
morality, 23, 29, 31

narcissism, 38–9, 41
narcissistic, 41, 43, 44, 121
Nash, A., 10
Nelson, M., 104
Nicholson, L., 130
nurturing
  activity, 46, 49, 70–3, 95, 123–5
  and agency, 14, 33, 38
  cross-cultural, 10, 70
  as instrumental action, 20–2
  and nature, 6, 17, 20, 35
  social location of, 17, 22–3, 81,
    83, 122, 124, 128
  and value systems, 3, 14–15, 19

obligations, 27, 29, 31, 122–3, 130,
  131
object-relations
  psychoanalytic theory, 11, 18,
    40–4, 73
oedipus, 38, 40, 41
  pre-oedipal, 38

Parsons, T., 13, 21–2, 26–8, 127
Pateman, C., 119
Pederson, F., 69
Piaget, J., 121

playgroups
  characteristics, 49–51
  normative context, 79, 81–4, 97
  venues, 51–62
politics, 124, 126, 130, 132, 133, 135
power
  of child, 9, 87, 105
  of father, 38
  and Foucault, 4, 16
  and Habermas, 30
  as a medium, 129
  of men over women, 128, 134
  and professional discourses, 126
  as a relation, 6, 9, 29, 104, 122,
    129
  of women, 130
primary carer, 64–70 *passim*, 79, 89,
  91, 95
public/private distinction, 17, 21–3,
  119, 122, 124
psychoanalytic
  theory, 33, 36, 37, 42
  conception of self, 34, 36
psychological
  literature on mothering, 16, 68,
    71, 93
  models of child development,
    10–11, 33
  processes, 44, 95, 115, 120, 121

rational, 7, 24, 25, 45, 120
rationality, 7
  forms of, 15, 29–30, 125–7, 135
  modernity model, 7, 133
rationalization, 120, 121, 124,
  126–8, 130, 131, 135
reason, 25–6, 28, 30, 121
recognition
  and autonomy, 18–19, 123
  mutual, 19, 122–4
  parental, 42–3
Reiger, K., 17, 73
remorse, 102, 106, 107
reparative
  discipline cycle, 99–101, 103–7,
    115
  form of subjectivity, 126
  guilt, 40, 41, 44
resistance, 16–17, 96, 111, 121, 130
Richards, L., 49

roles, 21, 34, 36, 38, 73, 83, 133
  role swap, 64–6, 82, 105
routines, 93–4, 96, 98
  see also care-giving behaviour
Ruddick, S., 15, 31, 32

Schaffer, R., 10, 68, 93
Scheper-Hughes, N., 12, 13
Schutz, A., 30, 31
self
  actualization, 70, 73
  assertion of, 18–19, 43, 70, 115
  constitution of, 33–7 *passim*,
    42–4, 95, 107, 115, 122, 125
  fulfilment, 14, 19
  self-interest, 23, 30
self-psychology, 42–3, 46
Segal, H., 40, 41
Shepher, J., 70
socialization
  and G.H. Mead, 34, 36
  mother's role in, 15, 35
  and nurturing, 20–2, 31–2
  theories of, 121–2
social learning theory, 33, 39
social psychology, 33, 34
state, the, 116, 121, 125, 127–31,
  133
  see also welfare state
Stern, D., 9
Sternglanz, S., 10
Stone, L., 130
subject
  as agent, 7, 25, 42
  of critical theory, 120
  as isolated actor, 28
  mother as, 18–19, 38, 46, 122,
    124
subject-object relations, 30–1, 86, 89,
  96–7, 99–100, 103, 114
subject-subject relations, 30–1, 45,
  99–100
subjectivity
  and autonomy, 6, 36
  child's, 7, 11, 19, 46, 95, 97
  construction of, 36, 94, 121, 132–3
  emancipatory, 7, 135
  forms of, 106, 120–1, 125–6
  mother's, 7, 18, 19, 23, 33–4, 41,
    122, 124

surrogate care, 104
  see also alternative care

Tiger, L., 70
Tönnies, F., 23–8
Trebilcot, J., 14–15

volunteers, 53, 55

Walkerdine, V., 15–17
weaning, 26–8, 77, 80, 98

Wearing, B., 14, 49
Weber, M., 26–8, 31, 120, 121, 125
welfare services, 134–5
welfare state, the, 128, 129, 130–1
Wilson, E., 129
Winnicott, D., 11, 141
women-centred, 4
  see also feminist value system
women's refuge, 134–5

Zaretsky, E., 130, 131